The Sanctus Germanus Prophecies
Volume 2

*The Lightbearer's Role During the Post-2012
Earth Changes and Reconstruction*

Michael P. Mau PhD
The Amanuensis

The Sanctus Germanus Foundation
Alberta, Canada
www.sanctusgermanus.net

To purchase more copies of this work, please go to:
www.sanctusgermanusbooks.com

Library and Archives Canada Cataloguing in Publication
Mau, Michael P.
The Sanctus Germanus Prophecies Volume 2: Earth Changes,
Reconstruction and the Role of the Lightbearer / by Michael P. Mau. – 3st
edition.

ISBN-10: 0978483545 ISBN-13: 9780978483548

1. Twenty-first century--Forecasts. 2. New Golden Age movement.
I. Sanctus Germanus Foundation. II. Title.
CB161.M37 2004 303.49'09'05
C2004-907016-9

Cover Design is taken from a miniature of an interior mural in the Bhutia Busty Monastery in Darjeeling, India that depicts the branch of the Spiritual Hierarchy which influenced this present work. The Great Soul, Guru Rinpoche or Padmasambhava, who emanates certain Masters of Wisdom, is surrounded by his disciples and Bodhisattvas or lightbearers.

Sanctus Germanus means Holy Brother and is one of the names of the Master of the Violet Flame in Brotherhood of Light. He is more popularly known as the Master St. Germain.

The Sanctus Germanus Foundation
Publications Division
Alberta, Canada

ii

Acknowledgements

I wish to thank the Himalayan Masters who so patiently worked with me during the early pre-dawn hours to convey their ideas that fill the text of this book. At every session I took down their ideas as best I could. But even when I did not quite seize their ideas perfectly, they patiently arranged a host of means to get the right meaning to me, including sending me up to the Himalayas for more meditation and guidance. It would have been easier to let them talk through me while in a light trance and record it, but they insisted on engaging my mind in this work, giving me hints and letting me search for the answers, all in the spirit of encouraging the practice of the conscious Amanuensis that Alice A. Bailey so pioneered in the 20th Century.

My gratitude extends to Micheline Ralet of Montreal, Canada for her diligent work in helping me proofread and edit the final text and to Matthew Thompson of Auckland, New Zealand for his artistic renditions of Diagrams 1 through 4.

Michael P. Mau
The Amanuensis
November 2006

Message from Sanctus Germanus

The enlightened of the day take one road while the others take another. But along each road lies a point where the two roads intersect. This is the critical point, for do you take the right turn and join the enlightened or do you continue down the path until another intersection is possible? Yes, these two roads intersect periodically and at each crossing you have a choice. So if this is the case, what is the rush toward enlightenment, you ask?

There is no rush in reality. Take your time. However, we stand here at an unprecedented juncture where opportunities abound—Earth has made Her decision to move on in Her evolution, and Cosmic Forces are preparing the way. You need not go along with Her, which means you may search for another galaxy and find a suitable planet at your level of evolution, where the living is comfortable and like attracts like. Ah! To be among those who share so much of the same! This is the comforting alternative, my friends.

For those who want to ride along with the Earth on Her journey into a higher dimension, hang on, because you're in for an exciting adventure! Yet there, on the other side of Oz lies the much promised land of the

Golden Era, and even if it is not comfortable getting there, the rewards will be greater once you arrive, for you will have also moved into a new dimension of promise on the road to your ascension.

So, my friends, it is just a matter of choice, isn't it? And a nice choice it is! But whatever road you choose, there will always be intersections of choice until your journey can be made hand in hand with the enlightened.

Master Sanctus Germanus

Table of Contents

Table of Contents

Table of Contents

List of Illustrations

PROLOGUE

For those who crave to see a better world, these are times of unprecedented opportunity. For those who thrive in the world as it flounders   today, these are times of misery and destruction. During these times, anything that does not serve mankind will be swept away, whereas that which promises to serve will be nurtured for the dawning of a New Golden Age.

These are also times of very clear choices, as good and bad flaunt their true colours. These are times when the march of events will both shock the unaware and delight the enlightened. The old is giving way to the new.

Like a freight train barrelling down its track, nothing can stop the dawning of the New Golden Age, for its time has come as inscribed in the Divine Plan. We must all come to the realization that we are now at the end of a major cosmic cycle that began hundreds of thousands of years ago. The clock is striking midnight; the finale has begun. Those reading this book will experience the upheaval of the finale's initial stages as crisis after crisis gains momentum and touches our daily lives. Never before will choices become so clear.

The predictions we presented in the *Sanctus Germanus Prophecies, Volume 1* are now coming to pass. The earth has entered the photon band. Higher vibrations are ever accelerating time and causing widespread insanity, testing the psyches of each and every one of us. A major financial and economic crisis pervades as the Dark Forces gradually lose their grip on a worldwide regime based on money and war. And before their final exit, another world war brews as those Dark Forces cash in on their last huge money-makers, *death and arms*. They intend to take the whole world down with them as they are forced to exit the planet.

To aid humanity during these troubled times, our planetary Spiritual Hierarchy has, since the 1940s, been bringing into incarnation hundreds of thousands of earth's past luminaries. Over many past incarnations these souls have contributed greatly to humanity's evolution in various fields such as music, art, science, religious thought, economics and politics. In this book we shall call them lightbearers, for they also make up the Army of Light whose aim is to counter the Dark Forces. By pre-arrangement they have incarnated around the world and represent all races, cultures, fields of endeavour and religions. They will serve as conduits of light to alleviate human suffering, guide to safety those who wish to survive the coming catastrophes, and plant the seeds of the transitional society that is to lead mankind into the New Golden Age.

Reinforcements and reserves in the form of the new root-race, the Sixth Root-Race, have been incarnating on earth in ever-greater numbers over the past decades. Their natural make-up enables them to see and function on the other planes of our existence, that is, the etheric, astral, and mental planes. How their natural talents are utilized for the implementation of the Divine Plan presents a challenge in the midst of chaos. The recognition and nurturing of Sixth Root-Race children rests in the hands of the lightbearers.

In addition, advanced souls have incarnated from higher planetary evolutions than earth, carrying with them soul knowledge that will help build the New Golden Age. These are friendly extra-terrestrials that the planetary Spiritual Hierarchy has invited to earth to aid humanity through this transition. They are here to work hand-in-hand with the forces of light.

Finally, the Spiritual Hierarchy itself is a formidable force of Light. It has begun to externalize onto the earth plane. Thousands of Masters and advanced initiates of their respective ashrams are focusing all their energies towards earth to help humanity through this transition. They represent the Planetary Logos on the earth plane. At key moments, they will manifest physically to carry out their pre-planned tasks or they will appear to those with clairvoyant sight to guide and advise them. They will serve as our ultimate reference points in times of chaos.

Now the battle between Light and Darkness is taking place, earth changes in the form of floods, earthquakes and land shifts have begun. The timetable for these changes has already been set, cosmically. What we do on earth will not stop their march. Whoever survives the battle between Light and Darkness will face even greater challenges, for just as we breathe freely again from the grip of the Dark

Forces, we will see massive natural disasters destroying most major cities and populated areas. Many lightbearers may then give up, but those who choose to fight on will lead survivors to certain Spiritual Regions and begin their REAL mission: society's reconstruction on firmer foundations.

In this book we shall focus on the Army of Lightbearers, who they are and what their mission is. Many of you who are naturally drawn to this book are lightbearers. We will 1) explore the lightbearers' role in the present financial, economic, and wartime turmoil, 2) define what is expected of the lightbearer as earth changes and natural catastrophes hit, 3) project their role in setting up Spiritual Regions for survivors of the earth changes, and 4) provide guidance to prepare lightbearers to meet the challenges ahead, starting now.

Our goal is to inform, not to argue or convince. As in *The Sanctus Germanus Prophecies volume 1*, published four years ago, we intend to present you with a banquet of information, foresight, vision, and esoteric concepts related to our times – food for thought, as we wish to call it. You may choose what to believe or what to reject. Ultimately the unfoldment of events will set the record straight and become historical fact. As the foreword message from Sanctus Germanus implies, what you decide to do or not to do in the next decade is merely a matter of choice.

Michael P. Mau
The Amanuensis
Montreal, Canada
November 2006

CHAPTER 1

Evolutionary Pace to the Golden Age

"Nothing in nature springs into existence suddenly, all being subjected to the same law of gradual evolution."[1]
El Morya

We have just entered a cycle that will eventually lead us into a New Golden Age of peace and enlightenment wherein the three major Paths of Evolution on the earth—the Elemental, Human, and Angelic Kingdoms—will again join hands. Mankind will walk with angels, seraphim and cherubim and benefit from their radiance and purity. We will also come to interact with the incredible world of elementals that gives form to objects, flowers, trees, lakes and mountains and precipitates our needs and desires.

As we move into this cycle, fetters that have bound mankind over centuries such as government control;

---

[1] Sinnett, A.P.The Mahatma Letters to A.P. Sinnett from the Mahatmas M. and K.H., transcribed by A.T. Barker, Theosophical University Press, Pasadena, California, Letter No. 14.

nation states; mass media; financial and banking entities and warmongers will cease to exist. By special dispensation of the Master Sanctus Germanus the root causes of mankind's imprisonment in this regime—the Dark Forces—are being cast off the planet, and mankind will rediscover what true freedom is; to expand, to grow, and to flourish.

Earth has faced similar junctures countless times before during its multi-million-year history. The last time this happened within recorded memory, the Atlantean civilisation faced similar choices, not unlike those we are about to encounter, before it sank into the Atlantic Ocean. Often depicted by Hollywood as an overnight disaster, the sinking of Atlantis, we are told to the contrary, actually lasted 700,000 years. So as we discuss the earth changes of the coming decades, we must bear in mind that these changes began centuries ago and follow the law of gradual evolution.[2] That we are only just becoming aware of them does not mean that from one day to the next our world will implode or explode.

We are not facing the end of the world as some dire predictions maintain. Instead, the earth's population will be significantly reduced and the millions of survivors of the coming changes will be given a second chance to right the wrongs of the past. As explained below, we are ending a lesser within a greater cycle of earth's evolution and from a cosmic point of view, this is considered to be just a minor period of destruction and cleansing, a Minor Pralaya, however it might seem from our perspective.

---

[2] Ibid.

Where Do We Stand Today?

More than one hundred years ago, Helena P. Blavatsky and Henry Steel Olcott founded the Theosophical Society under the guidance of the Masters Morya and Kuthumi. One of the Society's purposes was to announce to both east and west the closing of the Piscean cycle and the coming of the New Golden Age of Aquarius, a process that had begun in the 1600s. For this reason, Madame Blavatsky is often called the Mother of the New Age.

Grand Cycle of Involution and Evolution[3]

In the 1880s, in a series of precipitated letters, known as the *Mahatma Letters to A.P. Sinnett,* the Masters Kuthumi and Morya revealed to the Theosophical Society a simple schema that illustrates the evolutionary plan for the monad[4] - from a formless spirit to what we know as the human being, then back to the formless. This plan involves millions of years divided into seven Rounds. Each Round is further divided into seven sub-rounds, and each sub-round is further divided into seven cycles.

---

[3] Ibid.

[4] The monad is that immortal spark emanating from our Solar God, Amon Ra, which carries the oneness and unity of the Creator but nevertheless incarnates in the animal and human kingdoms and thus appears separate. This forms the illusionary paradox, for deep inside the incarnated being is the spark of unity.

Seven Rounds of the Evolutionary Plan

In Diagram 1 below, the Grand Cycle is divided into seven Rounds. The monad starts in Round I, then "descends" gradually down through Rounds II, III, and IV, before "ascending" the Cycle through Rounds V to VII. At the end of the Grand Cycle the monad regains its formless state but is much wiser having spent millions of years transiting this mighty school.

Each Round lasts about 2.5 billion years and involves a different planet in completion. For instance, Round IV represents Earth's tenure as host to the monad; Round V is Venus' and so forth. After many millions of years, Earth will complete Round IV and self-destruct. The same is true for Venus when it completes Round V. After each self-destruction, the monad will wait in limbo before "boarding" a new planet in the following Round.

When the monad "boarded" Earth, it also created its first form, which is referred to as the soul, causal body or Higher Self. [5] The causal body then delved deeper into denser matter to form the mental, astral, and etheric bodies of human beings before finally ending up in the physical body.

---

[5] From hereon, we will use these terms interchangeably

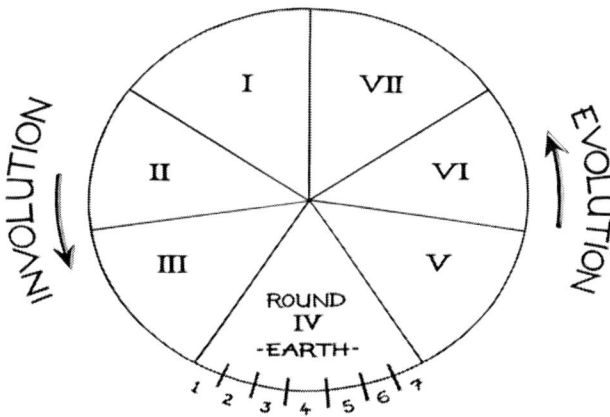

Diagram 1: The Monad's Long Journey through the
Seven Rounds[6]

The Master Morya describes the Monad's journey
through the Seven Rounds as follows:

1st Round —The monad is an ethereal being
— non-intelligent, but super-spiritual. As its
evolution proceeds, it will grow more and more
into an encased or incarnate being, but still
preponderantly ethereal. During this Round, it
develops monstrous bodies corresponding to its
coarse surroundings, as do the animals and
vegetables.

2nd Round — (After a period of pralaya,) the
monad lands on another planet. Its form is still

_____

[6] The Master Djwal Khul, then an advanced initiate of the
Master Kuthumi, drew the basic diagram, and we have
added some explanatory notes to make it clearer.

gigantic and ethereal, but grows firmer and more condensed in body — a more physical man, yet still less intelligent than spiritual. The development of mind matter is a slower and more difficult evolution than the physical frame.

3rd Round — On yet another planet, the monad is now encased in some sort of concrete or compacted body; at first the form of a giant ape, and more intelligent (or rather cunning) than spiritual. For in the downward arc of the Grand Cycle, he has now reached the point where his primordial spirituality is eclipsed or over-shadowed by nascent mentality. During the last half of this third round his gigantic stature decreases, his body improves in texture and he becomes a more rational being — though still more an ape than a Deva man.

4th Round and the Planet Earth — Intellect has an enormous development in this round. The races on earth acquire human speech. Language is perfected and knowledge in physical things increases. In the first half of Round IV, sciences, arts, literature and philosophy are born in one civilisation and reborn in another, civilisation and intellectual development taking place in cycle after cycle. By the halfway point of Round IV, Humanity teems with intellectual activity but its spiritual activities decrease. During the second half of Round IV, the spiritual Ego will begin its real struggle with body and mind to manifest its transcendental powers.

5th Round. — The same relative development, and the same struggle continues.

6th Round.
7th Round.
Of these we need not speak.[7]

Round IV and the Earth

Let us now focus on Round IV, which is our prime concern today. Like the other Rounds, it is divided into seven sub-rounds. As the monad with its causal body passed through the sub-Rounds, it began taking on progressively refined humanoid forms from cave man to the refined bodies with intellect that we have today.

We are currently completing Round IV's Fourth Sub-Round (see arrow in Diagram 2 below), which is at the very bottom of the Grand Cycle and represents the densest material form that the monad will ever experience. In other words, **we have hit the bottom of the Grand Cycle and from now on, the only way is UP!** This is why so many spiritual groups today are talking about Ascension; we have reached the turning point and the beginning of the upward climb.

Humanity will remain on Earth until we have completed the last three Sub-Rounds of Round IV. By that time we will have discarded our physical bodies in favour of etheric bodies. At the end of Round IV, Earth will self-destruct and we will move on to Round V on another planet. Venus is currently the planet of Round V monads so it is there we earthlings are headed. Indeed, the Planetary Logos of Earth's Spiritual Hierarchy, Sanat Kumara, comes from Venus,

---

[7] Ibid., Supplemental Notes with minor editing by the author

and our Spiritual Hierarchy often seeks advice from the Venusians.

Major and Minor Pralayas: Periods of Destruction and Rest

Major Pralayas within the Grand Cycle

A Major Pralaya, or period of obscuration or destruction, follows each Round. The next Major Pralaya will take place many millions of years from now, when Round IV comes to an end. At that time, our Earth will self-destruct[8] and we, the journeying monads, will retire to another dimension and rest while a new planet prepares to host us.

Today, many religious pundits speak of the "End Times" as if the earth was going to self-destruct by entering a Major Pralaya. Our position is that mankind is millions of years away from this fate. However, during those millions of years, mankind will have to endure three Minor Pralayas, including the one we are currently about to enter.

In diagram 2 below, we have indicated the Major Pralayas between Rounds. In reality, the Major Pralayas should be the same size as the Rounds because the duration of a Major Pralaya is said to be equal to the duration of its Round.

We show the Major Pralayas merely as a matter of information. What concerns us most today is the Minor Pralaya we are about to enter, which is indicated by the arrow in diagram 2 below.

---

[8] Our moon is said to be one of the disintegrating planets.

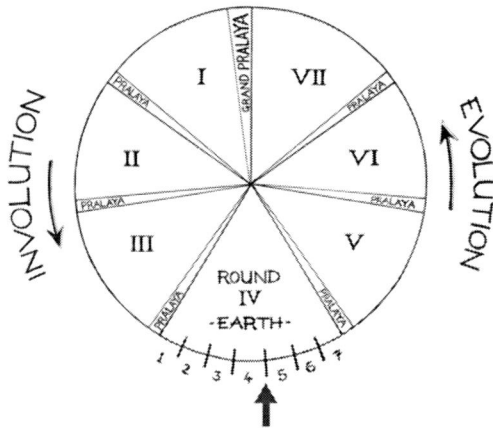

Diagram 2: Rounds, Major & Minor Pralayas
(Arrow points to the Minor Pralaya where we are now, at the
end of the Fourth Sub-Round)

Minor Pralayas within a Round

Minor Pralayas occur between sub-rounds. In Diagram 2 above, the arrow points to a line, which represents a Minor Pralaya at the end of the Fourth Sub-Round. This is where we stand today. During this Pralaya, the planet does not self-destruct but undergoes a cleansing or change in its geological make-up while survivors harbour in safe regions. Toward the end of the pralaya, they venture out into the remaining newly formed areas.

The term, Minor Pralaya, is, of course, relative and depends from which vantage point one is observing. From our earthly point of view, the current Minor Pralaya might look catastrophic with major flooding and sinking and rising continents that can alter landmass configuration and land to water ratio. For example, during the previous Minor Pralaya between Round IV's Third and Fourth Sub-Rounds the earth witnessed the sinking of the Atlantean continent into the Atlantic Ocean and the rising of the North American continent. Previous to that Minor Pralaya between the Second and Third Sub-Rounds, the massive Lemurian continent that stretched from the Indian subcontinent to north of Hawaii in the Pacific Ocean, sank.

The duration of a Minor Pralaya can vary. We are told, however, that the Hierarch of the New Golden Age, the Master Sanctus Germanus, has been allotted an extra amount of energy to accelerate the present Minor Pralaya because earth's evolution is presently behind schedule on the cosmic calendar due to the undue influence and domination of the Dark Forces and other laggard souls from lower evolutions.

Evolution of the Root-Races During the Round IV on Earth

So the monad enters its most material and densest physical vehicle of expression during Round IV. This physical form is expressed through the seven successive root-races that will appear during that Round. The seven Round IV root-races provide the genetic material for the physical bodies that the evolving monad will wear. With each successive root-race, there is a gradual refinement of the physical body in tandem with its monad-soul's evolution.

Each root-race further expresses its characteristics through seven sub-root-races. For instance, our present Fifth Root-Race's primary characteristic is the ability to think concretely as intelligence is firmly embodied in matter. The fifth and sixth sub-root races of the Fifth Root-Race are now in incarnation.

The entry and exit of a root-race leapfrogs Minor Pralayas so that the number of the sub-round does not correspond fully to the number of the root-race. (See diagram 3 below) For instance, the Fourth Root-Race began in the middle of the Third Sub-Round and survived until the middle of the Fourth Sub-Round. Our present Fifth Root-Race appeared in the middle of the Fourth Sub-Round and will survive until the middle of the Fifth Sub-Round. So the number assigned to the root-race does not necessarily correspond to the number of the sub-round.

Usually, when a root-race reaches its peak, a Minor Pralaya interrupts its development. This checks the excesses of the prevailing root-race, enabling it to retrace and correct some of its errors. At this time, our Fifth Root-Race has reached its peak, and the present Minor Pralaya will check its development before it gets out of hand.

While a prevailing root-race is in full swing, the next will begin to appear. Presently, many vanguard Sixth Root-Race incarnations are already appearing although the Fifth Root-Race prevails. These incarnations will increase during and after the present Minor Pralaya. So there is an overlapping of root-races as a previous root-race begins to decline.

SUB-ROUNDS
ROOT-RACES OF IV ROUND

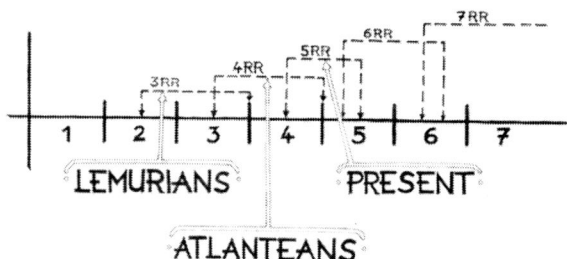

Diagram 3: Root-Races as they leap-frog between Sub-Rounds

The Fourth Root-Race began incarnating in the middle of Third Sub-Round. This was the Atlantean Civilisation. It reached its peak in time to be cut down by a Minor Pralaya that occurred between the Third and Fourth Sub-Rounds. During this Minor Pralaya, Atlantis' huge continent sunk while North America emerged. However, remnants of the Atlantean civilisation survived and certain souls of that period have persisted to incarnate well into the heyday of our Fifth Root-Race. Some are Dark Forces, to be expelled during the present Minor Pralaya.

So today we have remnants of the Fourth Root-Race, our dominant Fifth Root-Race, and the incoming Sixth Root-Race living on earth.

* * *

This brief description, based on the schema the Masters gave us almost a century ago, indicates that the Minor Pralaya we are presently entering, whether we refer to these times as the Armageddon, earth changes or anything else, should take place over an extended length of time, most likely centuries. This would indicate that there will not be an abrupt shift of the earth's axis and that if there is such a shift, it will occur at an evolutionary pace. In other words, we are not nearing the end of the world.

However, this is not to downplay the natural and man-made catastrophes we are about to experience, for these will be major upheavals the likes of which our root-race has never before experienced. Once the destructive first phase of our present Minor Pralaya has been accomplished, we may also look forward to the benign period of *rest*, which forms part of a pralaya, and it is during this rest period that the New Golden Age will come into manifestation.

Many reading this book will not live to see the end of the destructive phase of this pralaya but will experience the first jolts, as the cleansing waters flush out pollution and flood over great expanses of populated areas. But many will be able to contribute to the initial reshaping of human society, which will occur in the interludes between these upheavals.

Other Ways of Describing the Present Pralaya

End of the Sixth Ray Cycle

Another way of situating our current period is as measured by the Seven Rays. Students of esoteric literature are familiar with this concept as revealed to

33

mankind by the Master Djwal Khul via the writings of Alice A. Bailey. Our Solar Logos beams seven predominant characteristics or rays to the planets of our solar system--in 2000-year increments for each Ray--to make a 14,000-year cycle.

These seven streams of energy represent seven different vibrations in matter that define and infuse all objects. These energies can be combined in an infinite number of ways, giving matter's expression its varied and colourful characteristics. On earth, while a particular ray dominates a 2000-year period, each ray is present at all times and is "managed" by one of the Masters of Wisdom of the Spiritual Hierarchy:

> **First Ray** Will, purpose, power, destruction
> **Second Ray** Love, wisdom, inclusiveness, coherence, magnetism
> **Third Ray** Active Intelligence, adaptability, creativity
> **Fourth Ray** Harmony through conflict, beauty, sensitivity, unity
> **Fifth Ray** Concrete knowledge, science, mind, analysis
> **Sixth Ray** Devotion, idealism, adherence, force
> **Seventh Ray** Order, ceremony, organization, group, magic

We are now ending the 2000-year Sixth Ray cycle of devotion, idealism, adherence and force, sometimes known as the Christian Era, and entering the Seventh Ray cycle of order, ceremony, organisation, group and White Magic. The Seventh Ray cycle is also known as the Ray of Synthesis and combines all the characteristics and sub-characteristics of the other six rays. The Master Sanctus Germanus represents the Seventh Ray, which corresponds to his role as the Hierarch of the New Age.

The major shortcoming of this particular perspective of our present situation is that it does not really account for the periods of turmoil in between Ray periods.

End of a Sidereal Cycle

Another way to situate us today is by location in a sidereal cycle of about 25,920 years. This cycle is roughly the total time it takes earth to pass through all twelve constellations from Aries to Pisces on the astrological zodiac. It takes about 2100 years for the earth to pass through each constellation. We are now completing our passage through the Constellation of Pisces, the last of the twelve constellations, and are about to begin yet another 25,920-year cycle with a two-thousand year period called the Aquarian Age.

Realignment of the Earth's Axis with its Etheric Double

Yet another way of explaining the coming earth changes is what is known as the "Shift". Esoteric author and journalist Ruth Montgomery introduced this term in the 1970s.

The earth's etheric double maintains a steady position in relation to the Sun and the Solar Logos of this solar system. This constitutes a point of reference while the North-South Pole axis of physical earth is said to tilt back and forth with the times. When the pole axes of earth's etheric and physical bodies are in alignment, civilisation on earth reaches its highest state of spiritual development. When it is out of alignment, civilisation sinks into a dark age. It is said that man's follies contribute to the misalignment of the earth.

Over a 25,000-year cycle, earth becomes seriously misaligned from its etheric double and then realigns itself. Or, every 12,500 years the physical earth's axis tilts away from its double's axis, then takes another 12,500 years to return into alignment. At the point of realignment, powerful energies will pour from the Sun through the earth's axis causing natural catastrophes of a cleansing nature before the earth can begin another cycle.

Shamballa, the mystical seat of the Spiritual Hierarchy, sits at the North Pole of earth's etheric double. During the present 25,000-year cycle, earth has been so misaligned with this that estimates put Shamballa at a point above Central Asia close to the Himalayas, instead of where it should be, under the etheric North Pole. So when both north poles eventually move into realignment, Shamballa will be sitting above the North Pole of physical earth instead of in Central Asia.

Earth is presently approaching realignment with its etheric double. When the two axes are in full alignment, the New Golden Age will begin.

Year 2012 of the *Mayan* Calendar

Another measurement of the end of the present cycle is winter solstice of the year 2012. According to *Mayan* cosmology, 2012 is the completion of a 104,000-year cycle composed of four *Mayan* Great Cycles. Many hysterical western esotericists have seized upon this date to predict doom and gloom, even though this date is virtually unknown to the vast majority of the world's population today, including those of our major faiths. Astrologically speaking, the *Maya*ns believe that on or about December 2012 the planets of our solar system will all line up with the Sun, and the Sun's energy will pour through them like a lightening rod.

One such *Maya*n astronomer stated that the "oceans will boil" on that date. Whether or not the oceans boil remains to be seen, but such an occurrence in mid-winter in the Northern Hemisphere, we believe, will result in significantly warmer winters in the northern hemisphere from thereon. This trend has already started and scientists studying the polar ice caps are alarmed at the speed the polar caps are melting. We can be sure that from 2012 onward, this melting will increase in speed and intensity and the consequences of this climatic change will affect our civilisation, as we know it today, significantly.

Confluence

There is a confluence of these different methods that suggests we are at the end of a major cycle of cosmological time:

1. The end of the fourth sub-round on the schema the Masters presented above
2. The end of the Sixth Ray and the beginning of the Seventh Ray era
3. The end of the Piscean era as calculated by western astrological pundits, to be followed by the Age of Aquarius
4. The realignment of physical earth with its etheric double

5. The end of the *Mayan* Calendar with the year 2012

So from many vantage points we can see that we are entering a critical period in our evolution, one that involves the destruction of the old and the rising of the new, the ending of one cycle and the beginning of the next. We are not about to be annihilated, and life will go on after the catastrophes with the promise of a Golden Age within reach.

Everything comes at its appointed time and place in the evolution of Rounds, otherwise it would be impossible for the best seer to calculate the exact hour and year when such cataclysms great and small must occur. All an adept could once do was predict an approximate time; whereas now events that result in great geological changes can be predicted with as mathematical a certainty as eclipses and other revolutions in space.[9]

---

[9] The Master K.H., The Mahatma Letters to A.P. Sinnett, Letter 23 B received October, 1882, Adyar, India: Theosophical Publishing House.

CHAPTER 2

The Battleground on the Astral

Plane

". . .(T)he astral plane is the plane of illusion, of glamour, and of a distorted presentation of reality."Djwal Khul[10]

In this chapter, we shall discuss the esoteric basis of the current earth changes which, both on the human and planetary scales, are a reflection of the agitation taking place on earth's astral plane.

Below is a quotation from the Master Djwal Khul. You are invited to ponder it or put it aside if you do not understand or accept it. It is a profound statement, that, when understood, provides the basis of why we must go through the deep human and physical earth changes that face us.

. . . . Heat and moisture are present in the production of all forms of life, but the great mystery . . . is how the merging of three (Cosmic) fires can produce moisture or

---

[10] Bailey, Alice B., *A Treatise on White Magic*,(New York: Lucis Publishing Company, 1934) p. 222

the watery element. This problem and this phenomenon constitute the basis of the Great Illusion to which the ancient books refer; through the agency of the combination, the enveloping *maya* is produced. There is, in reality, no such thing as water; the water sphere, the astral plane, is, . . . an illusory effect and has no real existence. Yet—in time and space and to the understanding of the witnessing consciousness—it is more real than that which it hides and conceals.[11]

Earth is the only planet in our solar system where water plays such an important part. 71 percent of its surface is covered by water, and much of the remaining 29 percent land, measured by continental shelves, lies under water.

The physical body weight of some organisms is up to 90 percent water. The human body contains 60 percent water, the brain 70 percent and the lungs close to 90 percent. About 83 percent of our blood is water, which helps digest food, transport waste, and regulate temperature. Each day humans must replace 2.4 litres of water, some through drinking, the rest from foods eaten.

In esoteric terms, water reflects the ethers of the astral plane. The predominance of water on the physical planet earth reflects the influence the astral plane has on human life today. As we will see, water will play a crucial role in the earth changes hereon and mirror what happens on the astral plane.

---

[11] Ibid., p. 612

Where is Earth's Astral Plane?

We all spend close to a third of our lives each day on the astral plane. During our sleeping hours, most of us travel in our astral bodies onto the astral plane to work or study with friends and colleagues. Most of us return to the physical plane with little or no memory of these nightly journeys. Some, however, can return with full accounts of their dreams, sometimes mystifying, frequently symbolic.

At the moment of death, we cast off our physical and etheric bodies, leaving the astral body to work its way up through the seven sub-planes of the astral. How long we spend on the astral plane depends on the kind of life we have lived on the earth plane and our level of spiritual development. So "the good, the bad, and the ugly" populate the astrals.

The illustration below depicts the five planes, or form bodies, of earth – the physical, etheric, astral, mental, and causal. The astral plane makes up one of the five. These are identical to the five bodies of a human so the drawing depicts the close intertwining of our bodies with the earth's. (There are two higher planes, the Buddhic and Nirvanic that link the planet and mankind to the great cosmic forces that are not represented in this illustration.)

Earth's astral plane lies beyond earth's physical and etheric planes and is said by some to stretch almost halfway to the moon.[12] Other sources maintain that the astral plane is around 10,000 feet thick. [13]

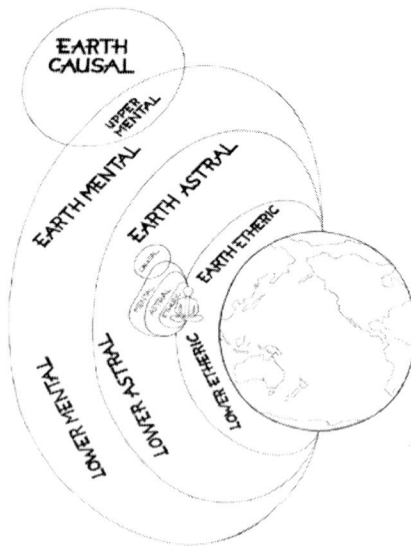

Diagram 4: The Five Form-Bodies of Earth and Man
Intertwined

The astral plane is divided into seven sub-planes and each sub-plane is made up of progressively finer etheric matter, working upward from the etheric plane to the seventh astral sub-plane. These progressively finer layers of etheric matter overlap each other so there is no clear division between the sub-planes, nevertheless each sub-plane hosts different populations of astral entities and represents entire conglomerates of ideas and thought-forms plus

---

[12] Leadbeater, C.W. *The Inner Life*, Vol. 1, Theosophical Society Publisher, 1910, p. 353.
[13] Innocenti, Geraldine, *Bridge to Freedom Collection of Channelings*, 1953

structures and institutions of similar vibrations. The sub-plane closest to the physical earth is very similar to life on earth while those on the higher astral sub-planes live increasingly ethereal and spiritual existences until they cast off their astral bodies and move into the mental plane.

The types of astral bodies that inhabit or transit through the astral planes are not mixed willy-nilly as on the earth; rather each sub-plane hosts astral bodies of similar vibrations. One could say that the lowest human criminal elements who pass over to the astral would thus be stuck on the lowest sub-plane until their souls undertake some redemption. Others who have lived more exemplary lives are grouped on the next sub-plane up and so forth. So the Cosmic Law of Attraction is very much in action on the astral plane.

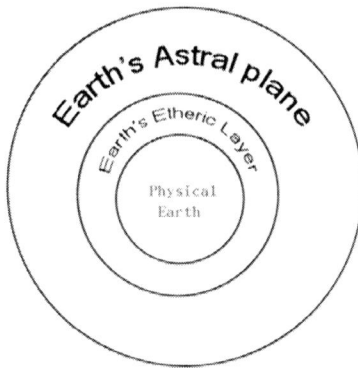

Diagram 5: Earth's astral plane

The ethers of the astral plane are liquid-like, which account for their close association with water on the earth plane and the fact that they are subject to the constant ebbs and flows of desires and the changes and whims of astral inhabitants, especially those on the unstable lower sub-planes closest to earth. The unceasing crises and emotional swings that sweep the earth plane reflect the movement and ripples of astral liquid.

It has been more than fifty years since esotericists have seriously studied and analyzed the astral plane and its influence on mankind. Much more research and observation needs to be done into this important aspect of life on earth, especially because of its wistful changeability and multi-mutations. However, the approach of the end to the Fourth Sub-Round of Round IV coincides with the Twentieth Century, with its unceasing war, mass media, and information age. These relatively recent phenomena have profoundly changed the nature of the astrals since the ancient sages and, more recently, esotericists have observed it.

> The appearance of the astral plane when first definitely *seen* by the "opened eye" of the aspirant is one of dense fog, confusion, changing forms, interpenetrating and intermingling colours, and is of such a kaleidoscopic appearance that the hopelessness of the enterprise seems overwhelming. It is not light, or starry or clear. It is apparently impenetrable disorder, for it is the meeting of ground forces.[14]

In fact, it is on the astral plane that the real battle between the Light and Dark Forces has already taken place and is now being played out on earth. We will see that the tenacity of the Dark Forces' resistance on the earth plane has its roots in Their virtual domination of the lower sub-planes of the astrals.

---

[14] Bailey, Alice B., *op. cit.*, p. 221

Present State of Earth's Astral Plane

The extraordinary events of the Twentieth Century have grossly polluted the lower sub-planes of the astral plane, forming a thick layer of tainted astral matter that colours pure thought-forms descending from the higher dimensions. Below we will demonstrate what this barrier is comprised of and how it has grown over the past 50 years.

Storage of Human History: Record of Astral Light

The astral plane stores its version of human history from the point of view of humanity's emotions: individual, group, and national aspirations; motivations; desires, feelings. This is called the akashic records of the emotional history of mankind. All of human invention-- art, literature, music, what modern day sociologists call "culture" and "civilisation", its fears, pleasures and anguish, its cinematic depictions, sexual desires, loves and hatred, agonies and ecstasies, inequalities, political battles, emotional swings of mass opinion, its aspirations (economic, power or religious-based), jealousies, aggressions, and so forth-- and everything else that characterizes the emotional nature of human existence is stored in the annals of the astral plane.

Whereas the mental plane stores all logical and rational thinking, the astral plane stores all thought-forms that arise out of desire and emotions. For example, a fashion wave may hit the earth, and everyone begins to wear jeans or a charismatic leader may organize mass political rallies to stir people to riot or wage war against their neighbours. Mass hatred that

45

pits one nation against another, one football team against the other, one religion against the other -- all are stored on the astral plane.

Each individual's emotional history - desires, whims, fears, hatreds, loves, etc - contributes to the mass of data stored on the astral plane through the intertwined link of that person's astral body with the earth's. Conversely, the emotions that bloat the astral plane play upon the individual's behaviour, often without conscious knowledge. In this way, we have national characteristics and aspirations that shape our behaviour and vice versa.

Thinking in Today's World

Much of the mental activity taking place on the earth plane today is of an astral nature, involving the saturation of people's minds by millions of fictional works depicting make believe characters and plots, the twisting of facts and propaganda dominating the media and its emphasis on broadcasting sensational or shocking events through our daily news and television programs. The information boom has created tons of fictitious books, magazines, comics and tabloid newspapers designed to evoke emotions. Cinema, television, and other audiovisual modes spread and diffuse such storytelling across an ever-burgeoning population at all levels of susceptibility.

It can be argued that, whether the thinking is fictional or based on fact, it is all the same, since it is all part of the *Maya*, or illusion, of the physical and astral planes. However, much of today's thinking has sunk to the level of entertainment and amusement, and the serious contemplative works characteristic of the mental plane have given way to the production of fiction and tragic, emotion-laden circumstances. It would seem most media works must have an "emotional hook" to sell or grab the attention of the consumer. Great thinkers and fine thoughts have been reduced to a minority, as the roar of the media muffles their voices.

The Mass Media and Information Age in the Twentieth Century

The mass media -- newspapers, magazines films, radio, TV, web, billboards, books, CDs, DVDs, videos, computer games and other forms of publishing -- convey astral thought-forms to the masses. Government propaganda, mass political conceptions, pop music, fictitious creations, literature, sports series and fashion trends, movies, the constant chatter and gossip of the popular media about movie stars, celebrities and the like all take form in astral matter on the astral plane before manifesting on earth. Aided by copying devices such as photocopiers, recording devices, video and digital cameras and computer software, these thought-forms are then multiplied exponentially and drummed into human consciousness until they penetrate and saturate both the subconscious (astral) and the conscious minds.

Mass media thought-forms originate from and return to the astral plane. The constant astral chatter of radio, TV, web, and movies shapes and influences mankind's thinking today and is without precedent in history. This is what we understand to be the broadcast powers of the hydra-headed beast depicted in Revelations of the Bible.

Our Economic System Feeds Desire on the Astral Plane

"The entire modern economic situation is of an astral nature; it is the outcome of desire and the result of a certain selfish use of the forces of matter." [15]

Starting from the creation of material desire through mind manipulation techniques such as advertising, we observe the millions of sea container-loads of toys, appliances, tools, clothes, cars, furniture, medical equipment etc. being transported from one end of the world to the other to satisfy human desires in giant shopping centres and stores in every country. Huge shiploads of raw materials—wood, metals, plastics, agricultural goods-- are bought and sold so that factories around the world can produce goods to satisfy every whim and desire.

Few, affluent or no, can escape the onslaught of these imposed desires, for they are eventually painted into our emotional or astral bodies either directly or through the mass consciousness. Add to this the exchange of trillions in bank transfers and cash to pay for the satisfaction of these desires and we have a global whirlwind of earthly trade-offs to feed astral desires. All goods, services and money exchanges have their counterpart on the astral plane, so never before has the astral plane bulged with so much manipulated desire and material satisfaction – or dissatisfaction.

---

[15] Ibid., p. 225

Mass Wars in the 20th and 21st Centuries Fill Astral Plane with their Carnage

The human carnage during the Twentieth Century has been without precedent. The two World Wars; Stalinist and Maoist purges, revolutions; wars of decolonisation, regional conflicts and genocides including the Korean and Vietnam wars; mass carnage in Bosnia, Cambodia, Congo, Sri Lanka, India-Pakistan, Somalia, the Middle East and so many more have overpopulated the astral plane with astral shells of the dead.

As previously explained, when a person dies, the soul throws off its physical and etheric bodies but the astral body continues to exist on the astral plane. If the soul is inclined to move on to the mental plane, the soul leaves its astral body and moves on, at which point the astral body goes through a second death, leaving behind an astral shell that will disintegrate over time.

If the soul is not inclined to move on – or evolve - as is the case with many criminal elements and lower type humans, the astral body will simply linger around on the lower sub-plane appropriate to that person's evolutionary level. All similar vibrations are grouped together, and many of the lower elements are becoming and remain patently bored with one another and thus seek vicarious excitement and adventure from the earth plane.

The violence of the Twentieth Century seen in the mass deaths of millions has filled these lower astral sub-planes with astral shells and entities, making it more impenetrable than ever before, to the point that it blocks the fine essence that usually flows from the higher spiritual dimensions to humanity.

Thus populated, the lower astral plane has gradually taken on a life of its own. Astral shells of bodies long gone, even dating back to the Lemurian era scavenge about preying on energy from the physical plane to put off their eventual disintegration. So loaded is the astral plane that it is said to add 150 pounds per square inch to the normal atmospheric pressure of 14.7 pounds per square inch![16] Is it any wonder that we feel we carry such burdens with us every day?

As we will discuss later, the Dark Forces have been able to resuscitate and recruit these hordes of astral shells and lingering lower evolutionary astral entities for their own purposes.

The Vampire Effect: Talking Dead and Resuscitation

Astral shells are soul-less and thus cannot draw their life vitality from their own souls as normal living beings do. Instead, as energy parasites, they depend on humanity to sustain themselves. They draw energy from group rallies such as sports events, religious gatherings, fundamentalist rallies, wars, and any other mass events that result in outpourings of emotions such as hatred or love.

---

[16] Archangel Michael's Discourse, "The Seven Beloved Archangels Speak", Bridge to Freedom, Inc., 1954

Individually, they may often possess humans who are unaware of this extra burden. Many astral shells retain unresolved obsessions such as alcoholism, drugs or smoking addictions and the like and draw the same experience vicariously by possessing physical bodies on the earth plane — a form of monkey –on-the-back syndrome.

Through such parasitical relationships, the astral plane has taken on a life unto itself. It has developed *self-interest*, for the shells have come to realise that they are on the road to disintegration and need a source of energy to sustain themselves. This, they can do both qualitatively and quantitatively by keeping mankind anchored into the physical plane.

Astral entities, desperate to sustain themselves i.e. stay "alive" have invented many ways of communicating with the physical plane and drawing the necessary energy, like a vampire, who is vivified after drawing blood from his victim. This is why, as the population of astral shells grows, Earth's physical human population also burgeons, for the astral plane must sustain itself.

Another means by which this occurs involves the possession by entities of individuals and organisations to create mass events, rallies, meeting, conflicts and wars—whatever is needed to feed and sustain astral populations. Astral shells of lower astral sub-planes, who have become pawns of the Dark Forces, are known to latch onto and possess individuals in order to force them to carry out their dark deeds.

At the same time, entities on the higher sub-planes of the astral plane, astral shells and thought-forms of past luminaries and inspired individuals, also sustain themselves by attaching to well-intentioned religious organizations and New Age meditation groups, posing as gurus or advisors from the "spiritual" realms. Most of what these shells have to say or teach is reiteration of what their human forms taught while incarnated on earth. Contrary to those of the lower astral sub-planes, most of these teachings are well-intentioned even though they do not come from the highest sources of wisdom.

So the parasitical nature of astral plane shells is both good and bad but generally no higher in spiritual development than the earth plane. For this reason, a parasitical astral relationship can appear to be holy, where it is in reality of a lower order. And such parasitical relationships are subject as any to the vagaries and emotional swings of the astral plane.

Extra-Terrestrials Promote Dark Hierarchy on the Astral Plane

It will come as no surprise to hear, then, that the astral plane has become the primary tool of the Dark Forces to broadcast and manipulate thinking on the earth plane. Hovering on the outer reaches of our atmosphere are extra-terrestrial forces hoping to profit from the chaos of this pralaya and institute their regime on earth. Even though they have allied with certain earthly governments, cosmic law still prohibits their entry into the earth plane. To access earth, they have instead learned to utilize the astral plane's inhabitants who, in turn, influence the human population on earth.

Agents of the Dark Forces in discarnate form reside in the lower sub-planes of the astral plane. They have no interest in ascending to the higher sub-planes or redeeming themselves and are therefore stuck *in situ*. Consequently, having no source of vitality, they seek survival through reincarnating, possessing individuals or influencing large groups.

The dark extra-terrestrials are able, somehow, to apply electrical technologies to energize these astral shells and bodies so that they can incite humans psychically to form groups and foster mass gatherings on the earth plane—this, in order to generate needed energy for their survival. We even suspect that they have the means to enable these astral shells to re-incarnate in flesh bodies, accounting for the great number of soulless humanoids walking on earth under the influence of the Dark Forces.

The New Age Movement Hijacked Through the Astral Plane

As more of the new generation on earth exhibit the psychic abilities necessary to communicate with the other planes, greater numbers of these untrained and uneducated psychics or mediums fall prey to astral entities masquerading as Masters or angels and expounding on various political or spiritual issues. These have been the source of a great deal of astral chatter, giving information of a lower, gossipy nature and urging receivers to proliferate information en masse via e-mail and the Internet. Every emotion they are able to evoke through these messages sends them extra energy and their tentacles extend more and more aggressively into the midst of mankind as their end nears.

The New Age Movement, prolific ashrams and religious groups offer ready access and sympathy to both ET's and astral shells posing as past saints and yogis. Astral entities and shells channel "messages from the higher realms" through untrained psychics in order to create large followings or ashrams as sources of energy. Highly devotional groups with blind faith followers are particularly prone to this type of manipulation through skewed interpretations of spiritual teachings, incitement to fanaticism and outpouring of emotions. As an example, the parading of the Pope's corpse among the masses to evoke an outpouring of grief must have served as a virtual banquet for astral shells.

Promotion of a Dark Hierarchy With Astral Characters

ET forces hovering about Earth have created a dark hierarchy that mimics the legitimate planetary Spiritual Hierarchy. The hierarchy includes facsimiles of Masters such as Sanctus Germanus, El Morya, and Kuthumi as well as others who have gained prominence through the New Age Movement. These facsimiles speak through hosts of untrained New Age psychics and mediums. Some even blatantly require their audiences to give them energy through chanting or certain sitting positions.

Even today there exist groups that have tried to revive 19th Century Spiritualist séance techniques in order to give this dark hierarchy a means to embody itself and communicate on the earth plane. Using ectoplasm emitted from their chosen mediums, astral shells have been able to make their presence seen or heard in the séance room. Their access to the Records of Astral Light enables them to impress their séance sitters with facts about their lives, and their spiritual teachings generally mimic the Ancient Wisdom.

As a result of Twentieth Century events and technological innovations, we can see that the lower sub-planes of astral plane have become a dark and murky layer of negative influence that blends with the earth's etheric plane and has for a considerable period of time impeded the flow of the Sun's *prana energies* to the earth plane. The general low state of health on the earth plane is just one result, mostly due to the emotional influence this plane plays on mankind, swinging both individuals and masses from one extreme to the other, much in the way a weather system can transform the still calm of the sea into a churning fury of destruction.

Cleansing of the Astral Plane

We have belaboured the description of the astral plane's present state chiefly to illustrate why, as part of the present obscuration or pralaya, the Spiritual Hierarchy and Greater Cosmic Forces have come together to cleanse it. Mankind, being the creator of the astral plane, has neither the will nor the power to cleanse it alone.

Cosmic Forces have now taken over, and an irreversible cleansing process has begun. Two types of Cosmic Forces are involved: The first is an inflow of finer etheric energies from the earth's mental and causal planes drifting down to the lower astral, etheric, and physical planes. These are feminine energies[17] that will balance the predominantly masculine energies of the present age. The second is a more general cleansing of all of earth's bodies as the solar system enters the Photon band of our present galaxy.

These two major cosmic forces affect all planes, and we are the most cognizant of their effects on the physical, etheric and astral planes. As they are of a higher vibrational nature, when they touch these lower vibrational planes, they cause the turmoil we feel on Earth before any benefits are felt. These are the forces behind the present cosmic filtering process popularly known as Armageddon (see volume 1).

Some individuals, however, through meditation and purification, have been able to forge a path through the thick astral matter in order to maintain contact with their higher mental and causal planes. By achieving this contact, they have surmounted the effects of the astral plane and thus can stay above the fray during the tumultuous cleansing process.

Downward Flow of Finer Feminine Etheric Energies

Corresponding with the timing of the present pralaya, the Great Ones of the Spiritual Hierarchy made the decision to release finer etheric matter from the mental and causal planes onto the astral. This is just one part of the dispensation gained for humanity

---

[17] Not to be confused with the female gender. Feminine energies are qualities that make up a certain category of cosmic energy.

by the Master Sanctus Germanus. These energies include the feminine qualities needed to balance the over-masculine energies pervading the earth plane. As the finer etheric energy descends upon the denser energies of the mental, astral, etheric, and physical planes it has a natural cleansing effect, as the grosser yields to the finer. It also has a profound healing effect on Earth's populations and will require a revision of science and knowledge to understand it. This healing effect has given rise to many energy-healing modalities in the New Age Movement.

As these finer energies extend down into the upper sub-planes of the astral plane, they will set the stage for the development of higher forms of art, emotion, and desire, which will further evolve during the New Golden Age. The continuing descent of these finer energies into the lower sub-planes of the astral will cause much upheaval as they come into conflict with denser energies. The main effect will be to drive the lower level astral shells and entities insane, which will be projected and reflected upon the earth as the general insanity we observe in current affairs today.

Specifically, as these finer energies reach into the lower sub-planes, the resident astral shells and bodies will foresee their demise, for the lower will yield to the higher. The finer energies will naturally hasten the deterioration of the residual astral shells and pulverize them into their original atomic or subatomic states. These entities will not, however, go down without mighty and desperate thrusts to survive, each thrust being perceived as a burst of violence or sudden insane behaviour somewhere on earth.

The great hope is this: No matter how violent the struggle, these astral entities will eventually be rooted out and allowed to dissipate, as they should have done in the first place.

Effect on the Earth Plane of the Descent of Finer Energies

The effect on the earth plane of these descending finer energies will be even more pronounced as the Fourth Sub-Round comes to a close, with astral shells and entities attempting to possess and drain more and more individuals on the earth plane for their needed vitality. School shootings by possessed individuals will become more prevalent and later branch out to other atrocities. Much of the increasing rise in drug and alcohol addiction can also be traced to these entities. They will possess society's weak-minded and disenfranchised to satisfy their unresolved cravings.

However, possession of the individual alone is not enough to sustain such a large population of astral entities. They must parasitically prey on larger and larger portions of the human population for sustenance. The best and most efficient way to draw energy from the earth plane is by evoking group fear-- the more fanatical the better, as fanaticism expends more energy.

Mass rallies and protests exude ever larger quantities of committed energy onto the astral plane-- the more emotional the undertaking, the greater the source of energy. The mass media with its sound and light technologies can easily create mass concentrations of energy. Worldwide sports events such as the World Cup and Olympics, rock concerts and rave gatherings, large ashrams and warfare, flashed into every household around the world through television and the Internet all evoke emotional outpourings that provide the astral plane with the energy necessary to sustain itself and resist the incoming energies.

By far the best sources of emotional outpourings are wars, the gorier and more atrocious the better. On the sidelines like the chorus in the ancient Greek tragedies, the media chants to gin up mass fears associated with war, pandemics, and terrorism in order to create even more sustained sources of emotional energy for desperate entities on the astral plane.

Large government institutions and bureaucracies, which have long been the "bread and butter" of energy supply for the astral plane, are slowly petering out as computers come to the fore. The tired, lifeless work style of the bureaucrat demonstrates how these older institutions have been drained of their vitality over the years. Therefore there is an urgent call to gin up new sources of energy in these desperate astral times. Since war represents the greatest expenditure of energy and can be mobilized by national governments, we will see more and more conflict in the closing days of this cycle. And of course, the hatred and fanaticism as seen in the recent Islamic and Christian movements add even more to this feast of emotive energy that keeps the astral plane fed and watered.

Eventually as these finer energies continue to filter down, the coarser agitation on the astral and earth planes will be tempered after the initial desperate outbursts, for despite attempts to survive, anything vibrationally incompatible with the new energies will disintegrate. Even the higher sub-planes of the astral plane will undergo a cleansing, and the quality of intellectual thinking, art and music will rise to a new standard in preparation for the New Golden Age.

Solar System enters the Galaxy's Photon Band and Agitates Astral Plane

Finer etheric energies are descending upon the various planes of earth at the same time the solar system has begun passing through our Galaxy's Photon Band (See diagram 6). This is not just a coincidence but part of the Divine Plan.

During this passage, the astral, etheric and earth planes will be subjected to powerful and turbulent energy bands that will have the effect of accelerating our perception of time and causing great turbulence, which will accelerate and aggravate the astral activity, causing desperate actions of self-preservation.

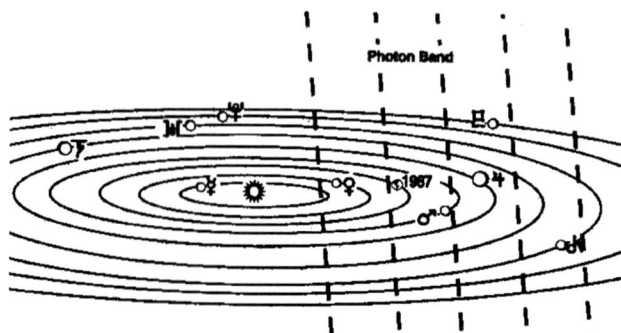

Diagram 6: Our Solar System Entering the Photon Band[18]

[18] Clow, Barbara Hand, *The Pleiadian Agenda, A new Cosmology for the Age of Light*, Santa Fe, New Mexico: Bear & Company Publishing, p. 37.

The Great Washer Effect

The combination of the downward flow of finer etheric energies and the "washer effect" of the photon band has a profound effect on the earth plane as astral shells and dark astral entities on the lower sub-planes closest to earth struggle to stay alive.

Diagram 7 illustrates the multidimensional, whirling paths of energies to which our solar system is subjected as it passes through the photon belt. Its effect on the astral plane can only cause turmoil to be played out on the earth plane.

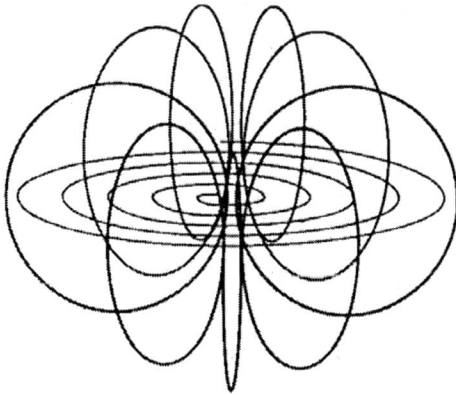

Diagram 7: Great Washer Effect of the Energies in the Photon Band[19]

---

[19] Ibid., p. 31

Desperate Reactions

As the finer energies cleanse the astral plane, the Dark Forces will lash out and try to drag the earth down with them by using the economic depression to justify trampling on man's rights and militarizing society. Their goal is to engage the world in a major war for which preparations are presently underway. This is the last hurdle for mankind and its association with the Dark Forces and should be perceived as the last sweep of the cleansing energies through the lower sub-planes of the astral.

These two major cleansing forces will continue until the astral plane has been cleaned of all that which does not serve mankind or earth. This will result in the collapse of the whole system of finance and warmongering that the Dark Forces have instituted to control earth's inhabitants. They will also be the force behind the vast earth changes that lie ahead over the coming decades and cause even greater upheaval in our present civilisation. These two major cosmic forces bearing down upon the earth will form the backdrop of all actions mankind undertakes from hereon. Mankind can either choose to buck the trend and perish or ride along with the pralaya and survive. It is a matter of choice.

CHAPTER 3

Earth Changes

"The approach of every new obscuration is always signalled by cataclysms of either fire or water."[20]
Kuthumi

Earth changes in the coming years will involve both fire and water. To translate Master Kuthumi words into modern terms, more heat on earth - global warming - will cause the meltdown of the vast ice sheet covering Greenland, the vast ice sheet continent of Antarctica, the permafrost in the northern reaches of North American and Asian landmasses, and the high mountainous stores of ice and permafrost in the various mountain ranges on earth.[21]

---

[20] A.P. Sinnett, op. cit., Letter 23B, Received October, 1882

[21] In the journal *Geophysical Research Letters*, a team led by Dr. Isabella Velicogna of the University of Colorado, Boulder, found that Greenland's ice sheet decreased by 162 (plus or minus 22) cubic kilometres a year between 2002 and 2005. This is higher than all previously published estimates, and it represents a rise of about 0.4 millimeters (.016 inches) per year to global sea levels. Greenland hosts the largest reservoir of freshwater in the northern hemisphere, and any

"Heat from the Seven Suns"

During a discussion about earth changes, a Tibetan Lama in the Himalayas echoed the teachings of the largest Tibetan Buddhist Order, the Kagyus, on what was about to take place. It is said the earth will go through the following three stages:

1. The heat of seven suns will bear down upon it
2. Heat will be followed by massive floods to cleanse the earth's surface
3. High winds will then follow to dry some of the flooded areas

This cycle would repeat itself until the earth was totally void of life in the case of a Major Pralaya or cleansed in the case of Minor Pralaya such as the one we currently face.

"When do these Buddhists expect these changes to happen?"

"Soon," he said. "I don't know exactly, but we believe it will be soon."[22]

To illustrate the possibility of the "heat of seven suns" bearing down upon the earth, Diagram 8 shows the relation of our solar system to other suns in the

---

substantial changes in the mass of its ice sheet will affect global sea levels, ocean circulation and climate.

[22] Private discussion with Lama Tenzing of the Bhutia Busty Monastery in Darjeeling, West Bengal, India, Novermber, 2005. This conversation was followed by a private audience with the Karmapa, the pope of the Kagyu Order in September, 2006 on the same subject.

galaxy and how at a given time, all seven suns could find themselves in the central band of the galaxy.

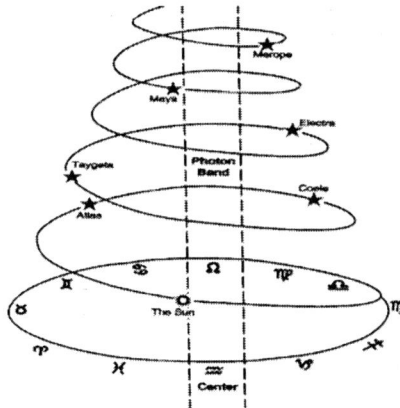

Diagram 8: Possible Coincidence of How the Seven Suns at a given moment in galactic time (2012?) could line up in the Photon band to produce the heat of the Seven Suns (each star represents a star with its solar system).[23]

Could the current alarming rate of global warming be the precursor of this great heat from the Seven Suns? We believe it is. In fact, we are already experiencing the effects of global warming — tsunamis, earthquakes, hurricanes, flooding — marking the tail end of the Fourth Sub-Round IV and the onset of the Minor Pralaya. Increased heat will be central to the earth changes.

In the years ahead we predict three stages of earth changes that will form the backdrop to the survival of human civilisation. For this purpose we will use the

---

[23] Clow, op.cit., p. 33.

Year 2012 as a convenient analytical marker for our time-bound minds.

No matter what path mankind takes, the earth changes will proceed, and mankind must decide how best to turn these changes into opportunities to create a better society, one that serves mankind in its quest for Soul Liberation.

Stage 1: The Present until Year 2012

Earth changes have been taking place for centuries in the form of volcanic eruptions, earthquakes, climatic changes, and the like. Presently, global warming should be of greatest concern to us. Up to the year 2012, regional or localized flooding, earthquakes and tsunamis will assail the earth. Coincidentally, these earth changes will 1) serve as a catalyst for the downfall of the current regime of finance and warmongering, 2) signal to lightbearers that they must prepare to move to certain Spiritual Regions in the highlands and 3) serve as warnings to the population at large of even greater "natural" disasters to come.

Stage 2: Earth Changes 2012 to 2080

We believe that in the Northern Hemisphere in the dead of winter 2012, temperatures will reach their peak as the Seven Suns momentarily line up and concentrate heat onto our solar system. Such an injection of energy will provoke even more rapid melting of the vast permafrost areas in the Northern Hemisphere and the continent of Antarctica, causing a significant rise in the sea levels, which in turn will gravely impact human society.

The accelerated meltdown will cause major flooding of lowland and coastal areas worldwide resulting in a mass exodus from low-lying regions to higher ground and certain designated Spiritual Regions. Amidst this turmoil, lightbearers will be able to seize this opportunity to create a transitional society that will lay the foundation stones for a New Golden Age. (See Chapters 6 to 8).

Stage 3: Continental Shifts 2080 and Beyond

Tucked away in the designated Spiritual Regions, human societies will experience a new awakening. Lightbearers and the remnants of civil populations will put into practice cosmic principles that will eventually usher in the New Golden Age in the Spiritual Regions, then spread to surrounding areas. At the same time major continental shifts will occur to change the surface of the earth for centuries to come.

Logic of Earth Changes

If we were to gaze upon the earth from the perspective of the Spiritual Hierarchy, there would be very few areas on earth's surface that mankind has not touched or altered in a negative way. The truth be said, mankind accounts for ALL the pollution on the earth's surface. Periodic cleansing to reclaim earth's pristine nature is necessary, so the earth changes we are undergoing are not random catastrophic events with no purpose or reason. From the perspective of the

Spiritual Hierarchy, they are cyclical as well as purposeful.

Since most pollution is located along coastal areas, inland waterways and urban areas, it is logical that these areas are going to be the most intensely targeted for cleansing in stages one and two. Areas of greatest industrial and moral pollution are where the greatest change will occur. Overcharged, heavily populated areas will be dispersed until earth regains its equilibrium and clarity.

The convulsions and cataclysms ahead are meant to cleanse and re-purify. They are not punishments for humanity, however much it might have caused the pollution. Should a cataclysm wash away vast numbers of human beings, this is because these individual souls have chosen to exit earth in this way. This is why we must emphasize that the individual's survival is a matter of choice. He or she can heed the multiple warnings and get out of harm's way or succumb.

Stage 1: Pre-2012 Warnings of Earth Changes to Come

Today we find ourselves in Stage 1 of an ongoing obscuration process that involves the 1) entry of finer, higher vibrational etheric matter, 2) the acceleration of time and the washer effect of entering the photon band, and 3) the increase of cosmic heat to produce global warning. We have already discussed the effects of both #1 and #2. Periodic catastrophic jolts from natural disasters will drain the resources of various would-be war-mongering nations along with further eroding governments' power and popularity as they bungle disaster response.

As the astral plane undergoes cleansing and the majority of the Dark Forces are expelled, we will begin to experience the brotherhood that has so long eluded humanity. The forces of the good and innocent will begin to outnumber the dark, negative forces, and the balance between light and darkness will tip on the side of the light. Group action and cooperation will reach a new high, and mutual aid and service will come naturally. The general atmosphere on the earth will be so much brighter, and the new glow will inspire all to revamp their lives, love their neighbours, and open themselves to the possibilities of higher dimensions.

But while we celebrate, we will have to face increasingly alarming signs of earth changes such as the rapid meltdown occurring in Alaska and Greenland and unusual weather patterns bringing drenching rains to other parts of the world. Unusual hurricane or typhoon activity in the Atlantic and the Pacific will result in greater-than-normal flooding of coastal areas and loss of life. These are the warning signs of greater earth changes to come, not just another weather cycle, and should spur people to begin planning a move to higher ground.

Warning Signs: Heat Waves, Storms, Polar Meltdown, and Earthquakes

Today's scientists are concluding that there is an "alarming" meltdown taking place in the Arctic and Antarctic regions of the globe. Global warming has now made it to the front pages of major newspapers. Headlines like "IT RAINED THIS WINTER IN

ANTARCTICA"[24] will dominate our news. Geological reports during the 2005-2006 winter indicate that the ice in the Arctic failed to re-form and that huge chunks of the Greenland glacier are falling into the sea even in winter. The meltdown has reached yet another plateau of acceleration. While mankind has added to global warming, blame and the good intentions of anti-global warming movements will not stop the meltdown. The scientist's "alarm" means that the obscuration process is now measurably visible and at our doorstep.

It is said that the Arctic Sea temperature averaged 23℃ about 55 millions of years ago and that the Atlantic reached 42℃ roughly 60 million years ago. This was the state of the earth then, and it will happen again. Heat waves will begin to grip the planet. Heat and relief, more heat and then relief will become the obvious pattern in the both hemispheres. At first, these climatic occurrences will grip isolated regions, then spread to larger areas, then to whole continents. These are signs not to be waved off, but to be reckoned with.

It is not only the meltdown of visible ice but also that of the vast permafrost zones in northern Canada and the Asian landmass in northern Russia that will raise the level of the seas and swell inland water bodies. Historically high levels of rainfall in regions around the world will be reported, and flooding will become more pronounced in previously arid regions. Dikes, dams, levees, and seawalls will come under more and more stress. Underground structures such as basements and parking complexes will be subject to groundwater seepage and water will start lapping on to

---

[24] *La Presse*, Montreal, March, 2006

walkways along lakes and coastal parks. Gradually, water will show signs of taking over the land, but in this pre-2012 period, most will be unable to connect these small occurrences to the greater picture.

In the pre-2012 period, violent hurricanes such as Katrina that struck New Orleans in 2005, the typhoons that drenched Southern China and India in 2005 and 2006, the floods that ravaged arid Ethiopia in 2006, the floods in Eastern Europe in 2005, and the 2004 Indian Ocean tsunami that struck the surrounding countries — these, and many other, climatic events were merely tasters of the future. In addition to big and spectacular storms, flash flooding, unusually heavy rainfall and "freak" cyclones will plague inland areas. Of course, scientists will mistakenly see these storms as the return of previous weather cycles such as El Nino or a 1930's Atlantic weather cycle, rather than as part of the initial process of obscuration.

Periodic underwater and land earthquakes will jolt us during this stage of the pralaya. Earthquakes will occur with increasing frequency and intensity where the earth's tectonic plates join. Again, these geological events are to be seen as warnings of what is to come but as they gain in frequency and amplitude, human disaster relief organisations will be so taxed as to be ineffective. The human toll in each successive event will increase, and governments will be exposed blatantly for their ineptitude and uselessness. People must understand that these early warning signs mean that they must start thinking about a plan of where to go and how to take care of themselves if they choose to survive.

Earth Changes that Accelerate the Downfall of the Dark Forces

Esoterically speaking, earth changes serve coincidentally as the Spiritual Hierarchy's trump cards. The financial house of cards that the Dark Forces (investment banks, stock brokerage firms, and the like) have built, in collusion with national governments, stands on the brink of collapse. We have entered a period of hyperinflation caused by governments that have flooded the world with fiat paper money from their printing presses that has no intrinsic value but that people attach to it. Never in the history of mankind has there been so much "liquidity" of worthless money. The derivatives market is particularly vulnerable to the slightest emotion-laden event. Tenuous "carry trades" like the yen-dollar arrangement between the Central Banks of Japan and the United States, bleed the world's financial system, transferring gargantuan profits to the coffers of the Dark Forces via their proxy investment banks.

Governmental collusion in these corrupt financial arrangements can be perpetuated because of the common man's ignorance of finance. These arrangements grow progressively fragile and the tiniest crisis will spark panic that will lead to a collapse of the whole worldwide system. The one thing the Dark Forces cannot control is a natural catastrophe.

Floods and earthquakes jar economies and government complacency and force attention more towards rescuing populations than engaging in corrupt finance and arms dealings. They are faced with evacuations and organizing relocations, funding repairs, dealing with unemployment, paying out benefits to the injured, rebuilding structures and infrastructures in new areas and much more. Natural disasters expose governments for the burden they are upon their populations and will hopefully awaken people to their ineptitude and uselessness.

From an esoteric point of view, earth changes will play a major role in triggering the downfall of the Dark Forces' regime and in educating the populations about what to expect post 2012.

Stage 2: Year 2012-2080: Increase of Solar Heat, Acceleration of Flooding, and Surviving Regions

Whether through the *Maya*n scholars' unlikely prediction of boiling oceans or the heat of "Seven Suns", heat will crescendo during the run up to 2012, and from mid-winter 2012 onward a greater influx of solar heat will accelerate polar cap and permafrost meltdown. This intense heat injection need only keep temperatures at the two poles above freezing during the winter months, and sea levels will rise accordingly.

Many of us will live to see the earth changes following 2012's intense inflow of energy. Most coastal areas will be permanently inundated and the world's main urban centres along coastal areas will be destroyed. Approximately 70 percent of the world's population (4.5 billion people) that live along and within 100 km of the coast will be affected, along with the millions living near inland rivers and water bodies, which will flood interior low-lying areas, splitting continents with inland seas and waterways. Most countries will be reduced in size or disappear under the floods. This will be the return of the diluvial era of Noah's ark.

The Northern Hemisphere includes the vast sub-polar permafrost region that stretches across the Asian landmass, North Atlantic region, and the North American continent south of the North Pole and is contiguous with the world's heaviest populated areas. The permafrost in the Southern Hemisphere lies mainly on the relatively isolated South Pole continent of Antarctica.

It is estimated that permafrost ranging from 50 to 1000 meters thick covers 20 percent of the earth's surface.[25] It exists at all altitudes from the lowlands to high plateaux and mountain peaks. The amount of water frozen into this vast zone is incalculable, but when melted could literally flood the earth.

For this reason, it is estimated that sea level will rise from 50 to 80 meters (150 to 240 feet) and flood all coastal areas. The countries of the Maldives and Bangladesh will disappear under water during the initial stages of flooding, followed by many low-lying countries like Belgium and the Netherlands.

The meltdown of the Northern Hemisphere's permafrost will inundate areas inland as well as on the coasts. For example, in North America, melting permafrost will drain into the Great Lakes basin that stretches from Hudson Bay to the five great lakes and will create a huge inland water body that will find its way to the ocean via the Mississippi and St. Lawrence

---

[25] "Permafrost," Ministry of Natural Resources Website, Government of Canada, 2006

Rivers. These rivers will swell to become inland seas that will split the North American continent into three parts. Other rivers and lakes in the western part of North America and south of the permafrost zone will swell and flood on their journey to the sea.

In the north Atlantic region, glaciers will melt to expose the pristine landmass that today we call Greenland. Its ice sheet is up to three kilometres thick. It is estimated that the melting of this glacier alone will add seven meters to current sea levels.

In the massive central Asian landmass from Norway to Western Siberia, the melting permafrost will create a vast inland sea bordering the northern tips of the Himalayas in what is Central Asia today.

In the Southern Hemisphere, the ice sheet on Antarctica's landmass is estimated to be about 4.2 kilometres thick. If West Antarctica continues to melt, the sea level will rise six metres. If East Antarctica melts down, the sea level will rise an extra 70 metres!

In addition, the extra warmth on the earth causes the water to expand more rapidly in the tropical and subtropical regions. And like a seesaw, land areas will also be rising up on one end and sinking on other, as they adjust to the lesser weight of the melting ice sheets.

Main Cities Permanently Inundated

The 70 percent of the population living on flat coastal plains resides in 11 of the world's 15 largest cities, located on the coast, bays and estuaries. Major financial and trade centres--New York, Chicago,

Seattle, San Francisco, Shanghai, Tokyo, Sydney, Saigon-Ho Chi Minh City, Singapore, Calcutta, Dubai, Dublin and London, will eventually be destroyed by flooding. The financial districts of Singapore, Mumbai, and Hong Kong/Macau sit on manmade landfill at the present sea level. Bangkok, Amsterdam, Rotterdam and New Orleans – and which of us can forget the sight of those levees - are barely above the present sea level.[26]

Large port cities located along main Northern Hemisphere river ways such as the Rhone (Geneva and Lyon), Rhine (Basle to Rotterdam), Mississippi (St. Paul, St. Louis, New Orleans), St. Lawrence (Toronto and Montreal), the Great Lakes (Chicago and Detroit), Yangtze (Wuhan and Nanjing), Yellow River (Zhengzhou and Jinan), Mekong (HCM City), Ganges (Dhaka and Calcutta), Indus (Karachi) will be inundated or washed away as thundering waves of water sweep down from melting permafrost at higher elevations. Major trade ports built on river delta areas of these great rivers of the world such as Chao Phraya (Bangkok), Irrawaddy (Yangon) and Niger (Lagos) are doomed. Most transportation hubs and routes—airports, rail lines and stations, highways, waterways—connected to these cities will also be flooded.

Massive earthquakes have always threatened Japan, but during this period they will generate

---

[26] The melting or displacement of Greenland's ice sheet would raise the sea level by seven meters, submerging coastal cities from London to Los Angeles. Just a one meter rise in sea levels would submerge Bangladesh and the Maldives, says Jonathan Gregory, a climate scientist at the University of Reading in England.

tsunamis that will strike the coasts of the entire Pacific Rim.

Oil rigs, pumps and refineries along coastal areas around the world will be inundated. Vast Asian hinterlands of Russia's oil industry will be subject to continued heavy rain, especially as the northern permafrost melts and begins to fill in the low-lying areas that were once inland seas. As the sea level rises, most of the Persian Gulf oil-producing areas will end up under the sea.

Broadcasts warning people to evacuate coastal areas for higher ground will for the most part remain unheeded. The majority of the people will unconsciously choose to remain and perish in the floods as their souls signal their departure from the earth plane. A relatively small minority will make their way to higher ground.

High Elevation Urban Areas Survive

Despite the massive losses along the coastal and low-lying regions, many high-elevation urban and rural regions will likely survive the floods intact. An estimated 20 to 30 percent of the world's population now inhabits higher elevated regions over 100 meters (300 feet) above present sea level. Although we expect levels to rise another 50 to 80 metres, the seas will continue to be turbulent, with storms battering the new and higher coastlines before the new weather system settles in.

Urban areas located on high plateaux surrounded by fertile land and with a good supply of fresh ground water will survive. These plateaux should be higher than large lakes and other water bodies.

Mountainous river valleys or narrow ravines and canyons, where flash flooding can take place, will be ravaged by melting permafrost, causing rivers to swell and temporarily flood these areas. Most of these high elevation regions can be found in the foothills of major mountain ranges.

Except for some Pacific and Caribbean islands and atolls, most countries with coastal areas have highland and mountainous regions. Barring earthquakes in those regions sitting between tectonic plates and the success of the Dark Forces in spreading pandemic diseases, the higher elevation areas should afford safety for many millions of people.

Some examples of high elevation regions and cities are:

North America: Boulder and Denver, Colorado, Salt Lake City, Utah, Calgary and Edmonton, Canada, eastern slopes of the Rockies

South America: La Paz, Bolivia, Brazilia-Goias in the Brazilian Highlands; Argentina: Córdoba, Capilla del Monte

Europe: Madrid, Spain; Pyrenees and the Ardennes-Alps region of Germany, Switzerland, Transylvanian Plateau in the Carpathian Mountains

Middle East: the Plateau of Iran, Turkey, Armenia

Central Asia: Afghanistan, Tajikistan and into the Himalayas

Indian Subcontinent: Simla, Darjeeling and Dharamsala in the foothills of the Himalayas and Ooty in Western and Eastern Ghats

China: Xian, Chengdu, Kunming, Lhasa, Tibetan Plateau; Qinghai-Xizang Plateau eastward up to the Da Hinggan-Taihang-Wushan mountains line, composed mainly of plateau and basins with elevation from 1,000 to 2,000 meters

Africa: Sub-Saharan Chad, Central Africa Republic, Central Highlands, Goma, Congo; Lake Kivu; Kigali, Rwanda; Kenyan Highlands, Uganda; Bujumbura, Burundi

Australia: the Great Dividing Range, Outback, Western Australia

New Zealand: All highland areas

There are high elevation areas on each continent where the basic communications and transport infrastructure will remain intact. Because these areas will be cut off from ground or sea transport, air transport and wireless telephone will serve as the only links between elevated safe regions. However, the state of these safe regions at the time of the major floods will depend on how they have survived the ravages of the deep economic depression and the world war.

Twelve Spiritual Regions

On each continent in high elevation regions, a Spiritual Region will emerge as a safe haven for initiates and lightbearers of the Spiritual Hierarchy to build a transitional society that will serve as a model for the rest of the world. Further details about these special regions will be discussed in the following chapters. These Spiritual Regions are:

North America: (1) Banff-Lake Louise area near Calgary, Canada to the Grand Tetons of Wyoming, US and (2) the Colorado Plateau

South America: (3) Córdoba Province in Argentina and (4) Goias Province in Brasil

Asia: (5) Qinghai-Tibet Plateau and (6) Gobi Desert Plateau

South Asia: (7) Darjeeling in the Himalayas

Australia: (8) the Australian Outback region

Middle East: (9) Iran plateau near Yazd, Iran

Africa: (10) Central Highlands Lake Kivu area and (11) the Ahaggar Plateau near Tamanrasset, Algeria

Europe: (12) Transylvanian Plateau in the Carpathian Mountains

Weather patterns on the earth will change radically in the coming decades in line with the greater availability of water and will make such forbidden arid areas as the Australian Outback, Saharan and Gobi Plateaux, much more habitable. Ethiopia, a very arid Africa country, has recently been under heavy flooding. A very mild, wet climate is expected to take over the earth, and regular rainfall will resume in arid regions that were once fertile and arable.

The Thirteenth Spiritual Region: Capital of the New Golden Age

The Thirteenth Spiritual Region will be designated the Capital of the New Golden Age around the year 2040. Two locations may be considered: Victoria Island in the Northern reaches of Canada or Greenland. What is revealed after the glaciers have melted and how these two locations are used during the world war will determine if either of them can meet the karmic requirements of the Spiritual Hierarchy for such a sacred location.

Nuclear Fall-out and Pandemics

The coastal and riverine flooding will inevitably affect nuclear power plants, since most are located near bodies of water. Nuclear radiation from flood-damaged plants presents serious dangers. The chance that Governments will take measures to deactivate these facilities at the behest of esoteric predictions is highly unlikely but man must always learn by his own experience and mistakes.

Another effect of these water-related earth changes will be pandemics. Some diseases will be born out of the release of biological pollution and stagnation in the aftermath of catastrophes. Others will be man-induced, for when the Dark Forces realize that they can no longer have their way in certain regions, they will release pandemics as part of their scorched earth tactics. In the aftermath of such pandemics, these areas will have to undergo years of cleansing before they can be used again for the New Golden Age.

Stage 3: Continental Shifts Beyond our Lifetimes

While civilisation struggles on, tucked away in the highland and Spiritual Regions, the rest of the earth will continue to undergo changes that will alter the earth's surface as we know it today. Many survivors living far from the Spiritual Regions are likely to be subject to these profound changes unless they are able to make their way to the Spiritual Regions and ultimate safety. It is unlikely that anyone reading this book today will witness these changes, but we can project the re-mapping of the world's surface into the New Golden Age as a matter of information.

Thousand Islands Scenario

The incoming energies projected onto the planet from 2012 onward will cause ever more profound changes on earth's surface, changes that will defy current science and logic. Whole continents will drift either in the same direction of the current tectonic plates, or certain landmasses will sink, as was the case with Atlantis, and some submerged land masses will rise from out of the oceans.

When all is settled, the configuration of land and sea expected for the New Golden Age will be large islands up to the size of New Zealand or Japan, interspersed by smaller water bodies. This will contrast with our present geographical configuration of large expanses of oceans and landmasses. No continental powers will exist. A world of a thousand islands will operate as a world without artificial boundaries. Water will serve as the delimitation of communities and the primary medium of communication between the islands, and sea transport in all forms will re-develop.

North American Continent

The west coast of North America from the Baja Peninsula to the panhandle of Alaska will detach forming several coastal islands. Earthquakes will cause one half of Alaska to drop off into the sea. The Central Valley of California, the Mojave Desert and low-lying areas along the coast will be submerged under the rising ocean and the Sierra Madre mountain range will constitute the new western coastline.

Water will create of the North American continent several large island-continents. North America will be split into three pieces: 1) the area west of the Mississippi, 2) east of the Mississippi and south of the St. Lawrence, and 3) East of the Great Lakes and north of the St. Lawrence. As the permafrost melts, the Hudson Bay will reach down to the Great Lakes Basin spilling over into the Mississippi to form a long seaway to the Gulf of Mexico and into the St. Lawrence to form an even wider seaway connecting to the Atlantic. The whole mid-west up to the Rockies will be inundated, and the Rockies will jut out as an island-continent.

The north-south range of the Rocky Mountains will be cut into segments by earthquakes and form several island-continents as the Pacific and the North American tectonic plates move in opposite directions. The foothills and plateaux on the eastern slopes of the Rockies will constitute Spiritual Regions for the surviving populations of the North American Continent.

Central and South America

In South America water will once again separate the Andes from the coastal highlands that run from Brazil (Bahia, Minas Gerais, Parana, Santa Catarina) to Argentina with all the central lowlands running from the Amazon valley down through to the southern part of Argentina being inundated. What is now South America will become two large island-continents.

All of Central America will be submerged, and the connection between North and South America will be cut off

Asia and the Pacific Rim

As both the eastern and western sides of the Pacific Rim rock with earthquakes, the resulting tsunamis and ocean disturbances will temporarily submerge most of the Pacific Islands, especially Hawaii. Then parts of the lost continent of Lemuria will rise out of the middle of the Pacific.

Most of China's lowland coastal areas will be submerged during Stage 2. Then, through a series of seismic movements, all that will remain of present China will be the high plateau of the Gobi desert and the Qinghai-Tibetan plateau, which will serve as the point of refuge for the Chinese civilisation. There it will again flourish in the New Golden Age under the original Chinese race as one of the Spiritual Regions.

The islands of Taiwan and the Philippines will submerge as underwater land masses rise out of the Pacific.

Southeast Asia

Most of Southeast Asia will be severely flooded. All the lowlands around the Tonle Sap Lake of Cambodia and South Vietnam — the Mekong Delta -- will sink with the higher areas of Laos and Northern Vietnam becoming a peninsula.

Central Asia

Russia below the 65 degree latitude will become a soggy marchland due to the meltdown of permafrost that will drain into a huge inland sea where the Western Siberian lowlands and the Kirgiz steppe are now located.

South Asia

India's lowlands, the Indus and Ganges river valleys will be submerged during stage 2. What will remain are the foothills and hill stations of the Himalayas. The Western Ghats will form another island-continent. The Himalayas and the Western Ghats will serve as two Spiritual Regions in which humanity will continue evolving.

Australia and New Zealand

Australia's eastern side will be submerged while the western desert will become habitable. New Zealand will be pushed up out of the sea to create a larger island-continent.

New Zealand and the Western desert of Australia will serve as the Spiritual Regions down under.

Europe

The British Isles and most of Western Europe, including the lowlands of Germany, France, Italy and Spain will be submerged. Much of Scandinavia will remain intact although its coastal areas will be submerged.

Eastern Europe's river basins will be submerged. The Carpathians will emerge as an island-continent with a Spiritual Region.

Northern European populations will find refuge in the Scandinavian highlands while western and eastern European populations should repair to the Carpathian mountain range.

A large island-continent will rise out of the North Atlantic Ocean between North American and Europe.

The Middle East

The Persian Gulf will become a huge sea covering Saudi Arabia, Kuwait and Iraq and stretching from Egypt to the western shores of India. To the north Iran and Turkey will flood so that the Caspian Sea, Black

Sea and the Eastern Mediterranean are all one body of water. There will no longer be any need for the Suez Canal. The whole Arabian Peninsula to the east of the Suez will submerge.

Africa

Today's African continent will split into four island-continents: 1) The West African region, the Senegal and Niger Rivers will separate from the north and become a large island. 2) Much of sub-Saharan Africa will be covered with water as high sea levels inundate the river systems and surrounding areas. The inland delta of the Niger in Mali will form a huge lake. However, the arid northern plateau of the Sahara will remain intact and form a new island-continent where a Golden Age once existed under the command of Sanctus Germanus. Heavy rains will rejuvenate this region. The inland sea that now lies under the Sahara will rise and join with the Mediterranean in the north. 3) What is South and Southeast Africa today will break away from the main continent to become an island-continent, and 4) the central highlands where Kenya, Burundi and Rwanda are located will remain intact and serve as one of the Spiritual Regions during this long period of continental change. Most of Egypt will be submerged.

Emergence of Pristine Lands

As the polar and permafrost meltdown advances, vast pristine lands in the northern reaches of Canada and Russia will be revealed from under the ice and used for the New Golden Age. Greenland will emerge as a temperate area with virgin lands exposed once its glaciers have melted.   These post-diluvian areas, however, will require many decades, if not centuries, to drain and become habitable.

Some islands, such as those in the Pacific with active volcanoes will rise further from beneath the oceans. These will manifest as large land bodies in the middle of the ocean and become island-continents. The present islands will become the future highlands of these island-continents and their rains will flow down for decades leaching out the saline areas. Most of these areas will remain uninhabited until repopulated centuries later.

Survivors of Stage 3 of the pralaya will be scattered around the world in various Spiritual Regions. We will discuss how these areas will bring in the much-promised Golden Age in the following chapters.

* * *

Most of us will live to experience Stage 1 and Stage 2. Many may choose not to go on after Stage 1 is completed, but others will be driven by a sense of purpose and mission to continue into Stage 2. These lightbearers have been placed on the earth plane during this time to inform and lead mankind as best they can through the pralaya. We shall now see who these people are and what tasks lie ahead for them amid all the earth changes.

CHAPTER 4

Role of the Lightbearer

". . . the moment a man can 'see' on the astral plane, and can achieve equilibrium and hold steady in the midst of its vibrating forces, that moment he is ready for initiation."[27] *Djwal Khul*

Amid the chaos of the present pralaya, the Spiritual Hierarchy has called upon the brightest and best to serve as beacons of light to a suffering humanity. These are the tried and true lightbearers, who have spent thousands of lifetimes making their long and arduous journeys through the initiations of the Spiritual Hierarchy. In this chapter we will identify these lightbearers, discuss the leadership role they will play during this pralaya and the current crisis of commitment.

Who are the Lightbearers?

More than four hundred years ago, the Masters of Wisdom and their initiates laid out plans for this current pralaya and the Golden Age that would follow. Since this was to be a Minor Pralaya of partial destruction, the Hierarchy decided to embark on an

---

[27] Bailey, op. cit., p. 221

experiment to give the present civilisation another chance to right its wrongs, reshape society, and prepare it for a Golden Age. Realizing that humanity would need all the help it could muster, the Hierarchy called for volunteers from amongst their own high-level initiates and from other, higher, evolutions to reincarnate on earth during this time.

The Hierarchy would rely heavily on the four levels of initiates as well as disciples and probationers on the Path to carry out the Divine Plan. Diagram 9 below shows the Planetary Hierarchy or the inner government of our planet and how it reaches down to the earth plane through its initiates and disciples. From the Lord of the World, Sanat Kumara, down to the probationer on the Path, the role of the initiates as intermediaries between the earth plane and the Spiritual Hierarchy is essential.

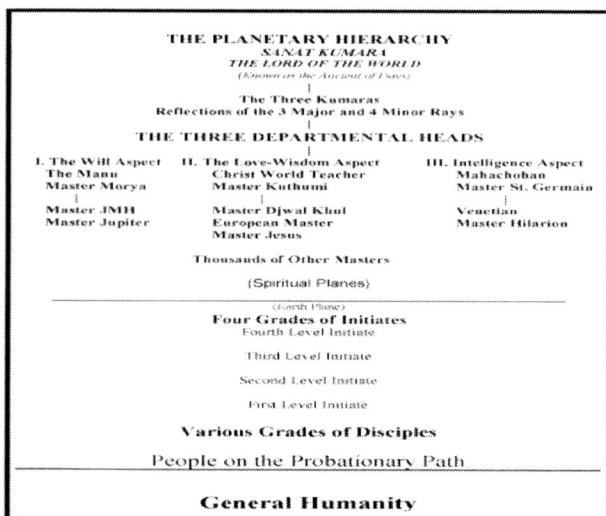

Diagram 9: The four levels of initiates on the earth plane and their relationship to the Spiritual Hierarchy

The Spiritual Hierarchy introduced the Path of Initiation to humanity millions of years ago so that humans could, through spiritual evolution, make their way up the ranks of the Hierarchy. Eventually, spiritually advanced individuals who had passed through earth's school of hard knocks would evolve to the point where they would reach Masterhood and occupy high cosmic offices in the Hierarchy. This way, the Planetary Logos would not have to rely on advanced souls from other planets to fill the ranks of earth's Hierarchy but could draw on initiates with earthbound experience. This is the case today, where most, if not all the initiates approaching Masterhood, and the Masters of Wisdom themselves, are products of earthly experience. At any time, there are thousands making their way up the Path of Initiation.

So, out of the pool of discarnate initiates on the spiritual plane, thousands volunteered to put aside their pursuit of individual enlightenment in order to reincarnate during this period of upheaval. They made this decision out of compassion for humanity and would be known on earth as *bodhisattvas or lightbearers.* Volunteers were presented before the Karmic Board, and one in three were chosen to incarnate.[28]

These volunteers worked closely with teams from all three Hierarchical departments, under the guidance of the Master Sanctus Germanus, to draw up plans for this pralaya. Many who had volunteered had already passed through the Fourth Initiation and no longer needed to incarnate on earth to advance. Some had already achieved the Second or Third Initiations.

---

[28] Innocenti, *op. cit.*

Others volunteered to reincarnate several times in the four hundred year period, in order to learn necessary skills to make them more useful during this pralaya. In many cases, it has taken at least eight to ten generations of incarnations for these souls to prepare for their critical roles in the years to come.

Those chosen were *la crème de la crème*. Never before in the history of mankind have so many past luminaries elected to return to the earth plane one last time to spend their lives learning and mastering a necessary field of endeavour such as finance, politics, banking, education, art and music in order to carry the positive aspects of these fields into the New Golden Age. Aside from acquiring professional expertise, sometimes in areas dominated by the Dark Forces, they would all share one thing: a yearning for the spiritual, no matter how difficult or easy the mission.

The Making of a Lightbearer

Throughout the many centuries preceding this pralaya, lightbearers have reincarnated hundreds if not thousands of times to learn lessons from earth's school. Over several lifetimes they consciously broke away from the masses, entered the Path of Initiation, and became servers of humanity. The process described below summarizes how they became initiates and chose to return to help those they left behind.

General Humanity ranges from the masses struggling to meet their basic daily needs to those of great wealth and material achievement. Spiritual development concerns them little. Out of the masses candidates for the initiation process filter out. Any soul is welcome to embark on the Path of Initiation by entering the Probationary Path.

At this point the personality begins to take cognizance of itself and moves to improve its weaknesses. Each time it reincarnates, it picks up where it left off in the previous lifetime until the soul leads it firmly on the Probationary Path. A guiding Master is aware of the soul's effort and assigns an initiate or disciple to watch over it. After several lifetimes on the Probationary Path, it produces a personality that achieves standing as a Master's disciple and becomes aware of working for group efforts rather than just for itself. If the disciple is fortunate to have money at his or her disposal, it should be used for the good of service.

After several lifetimes the soul is ready to enter the Portal of Initiation. Several lifetimes are spent on the First Initiation, as the soul grapples to bring the physical body and its desires under control. It then passes onto the Second Initiation, where the soul brings the astral body under control. Then comes the Third Initiation (Transcendence) where the initiate learns to control his mental vehicle and manipulate thought matter. Both the second and third initiations can be achieved within one lifetime. Finally, comes the Fourth Initiation (Crucifixion), where the lightbearer is in reality an adept who has mastered the physical, etheric, astral, and mental bodies and even reaches into the two lower sub-planes of his Buddhic vehicle. After the Fourth Initiation, the soul is no longer required to reincarnate on the earth plane. Both the Third and Fourth Initiations are conferred by Sanat Kumara Himself. [29]

The Masters of Wisdom know the soul history of each and every lightbearer; their akashic records being stored in Shamballa's Hall of Records. The Spiritual Hierarchy is thus solely in the position to initiate individuals, having the full history of soul at their disposal. To date, there are no human organisations on the earth plane authorized or capable of initiating disciples in the name of the Hierarchy. Yet many New Age organisations administer attunements or initiations, promise rapid formulae for ascension and purport to carry out Hierarchical initiation ceremonies. These are grossly misleading many well-intentioned lightbearers who seek only to retrieve their soul plans. However, if lightbearers allow themselves to be misled, they then will prove themselves unfit for true service to the Hierarchy.

The Lightbearers of Today

No matter how advanced the initiates may be at the time of their reincarnation, once incarnated they are subject to the memory veil that blocks all previous knowledge and soul plans from consciousness. This is the level playing field, so to speak, until the lightbearer realises his or her path and re-discovers the plan he or she has laid out.

As part of the Divine Plan, lightbearers have returned to earth to accomplish a mission rather than

---

[29] For more information on the Path of Initiation, consult Alice A. Bailey's *Initiation Human and Solar*, Lucis Trust, New York.

achieve sainthood. We make this statement in a bit of jest, because to accomplish their missions, they must also possess many of the qualities of "Sainthood". All lightbearers spent previous lives in some form of self-abnegation, sacrifice, and purity in service to humanity on the road to achieving soul integration with the personality. Many also contributed to mankind's advancement through their scientific and artistic breakthroughs. Some were statespersons whose policies and perseverance liberated their fellow humans from political as well as other forms of oppression. Some worked tirelessly to relieve human suffering and contributed many positive works to humanity with great personal sacrifice. From their past lives, their souls are geared to service to mankind.

Back again this time, many lightbearers suffer greatly during childhood, primarily because they choose to balance any residual karma early on before entering into full service of the Hierarchy during the pralaya. They often choose families where they suffer psychological or physical abuse, for childhood is like boot camp for the lightbearer. They often do not fit in with their families and indeed some do not even physically resemble their biological parents. Within the family, they stand out as different or even black sheep.

They may also suffer in normal educational institutions because they tend not to conform to the normal rites of growing up. Being tried and true matured souls, they often do not see the need to be part of the silliness that pervades secondary education. Their fellow classmates often consider them social outcasts and as a result they suffer from loneliness. However, they are likely to excel academically. Their inner strength sustains them through the painful growing-up period, and many begin to find inner and professional strength once they are independent from their families.

Many lightbearers will reject traditional religions early on because they have already surpassed the limitations of dogma in previous lives. Others opt for working within established traditional religions as reformers, rebels or innovators. However, many choose to remain spiritually neutral and unaffiliated with traditional religious movements.

As many reach the zenith of their professional careers, their spiritual yearnings become more and more intense. Some leave their posts while others struggle to maintain interest in their jobs and still answer the spiritual yearnings within. A search begins. They begin to look for answers in the other dimensions, consulting astrologers, psychics, and mediums; poring through books on near-death experiences; or visiting the many spiritually oriented websites on the Internet. Some questions are answered, but inevitably they are left with more questions than answers. At this juncture, it is usually time for the lightbearer to begin the retrieval of his or her last initiation.

Retrieval of the Last Initiative Level[30]

In all lightbearers plans, there is a trigger that should awaken them to a deep feeling that they need to fulfill some kind of spiritual mission. This awakening should take place in the years leading up to 2012. The

---

[30] See Chapter 5

trigger could be a deep emotional crisis, a growing dissatisfaction with life in general or a simple, all-abiding knowledge that priorities in one's life have got to change. Life just "doesn't feel right" and seems to be butting against a brick wall.

As this awakening needles the lightbearer, he or she feels the nudge to look into the spiritual side of life, and there begins a gradual process of reversing life priorities, probing into spiritual teachings and re-contacting the soul until the spiritual life becomes more important than the professional. Following the urgings of this awakening requires that the lightbearer re-establish contact with the Higher Self and in doing so, he or she re-connects to the Divine Plan.

Usually, the retrieval involves a rapid retake of all the arduous steps from probation to discipleship and then to the initiations themselves. Through deep meditation, study, and service, this fast-forward path to initiation can be achieved within a few years rather than several lifetimes. The process can be quite trying, as it demands a quickening of the vibrations of the body vehicle, so much so that sometimes, the body is too weak to withstand the rapid transformations. However, this process takes place under the supervision of a Master.

As the lightbearer retrieves the initiation process in condensed form, he or she must also deal with all the bad habits and karma picked up during the present incarnation.

Retrieval can be both invigorating and earthshaking to the personality, so many lightbearers fall by the wayside and give up.

Those who successfully retrieve their previous level of initiation may have to re-learn how to serve humanity. Service is written into the lightbearer's soul, but life's circumstances and the personality can obscure its manifestation. Usually the lightbearer's professional expertise is related to this divine service, but not until reconnection with one's Higher Self has taken place can the lightbearer's expertise be placed in the overall local and world context.

Alternative to Retrieval

The Spiritual Hierarchy has used another arrangement to bring into incarnation past luminaries or advanced initiates who are busy with other projects in the spiritual dimensions. Another soul will volunteer to incarnate and prepare a body vehicle from birth until a given time, usually an emotional crisis, at which point the first soul will vacate the body and another, more advanced, will take its place. As the first soul gradually vacates, the personality either experiences a rub with death or psychologically wishes to die. This is an indication of a walk-in replacement.

The body vehicle retains all the education, breeding, and memories of the former soul, and except for subtle differences in personality, the walk-in soul is usually unperceived except by those who know the person intimately or by other walk-ins. The body is reinvigorated by the new vital energy and pursues the mission defined by its new soul. It will however still experience a period of physical adjustment, which can be trying and uncomfortable.

The Successful Retrieval or Walk-in

As more advanced lightbearers retrieve their former initiation levels and walk-ins settle into their new body vehicles, they become aware of or unlock former abilities as White Magicians. As these abilities emerge through the personality, they are directed toward the context of the pralaya and the upheavals to come. As lightbearers regain their status as White Magicians, they can do the most good during these trying times. Having an understanding of the context of the earth changes, they are able to become spokespersons for the Spiritual Hierarchy, explaining to their neighbours and friends the reasons for the upheavals and presenting this information to the general public, to their families, friends, and colleagues as food-for-thought.

It is not uncommon for the majority of humanity to balk at and resist this information; perhaps even aggressively argue against it; new ideas that disturb preconceived notions are bound to cause discomfort, resistance to change being one of our hallmarks. Lightbearers will find themselves accused of being purveyors of negativity and prophets of doom because the public will not want to hear anything that upsets the status quo. At the same time, violent, catastrophic earth changes and turmoil may touch the lightbearer's community, causing many to wake up: eventually the lightbearer will be able to emerge as a sane leader in the midst of the insanity.

Because of the urgent context we find ourselves in today, it is not uncommon for reconnected lightbearers to experience an "upgrade" in initiation status, more commonly earned by going through the rapid and often painful retrieval process.

A Crisis of Commitment

The years 2006 to 2007 coincide with a sharp dismantling of the financial markets, which will touch everyone. The Spiritual Hierarchy estimates that lightbearers should by this time have come to a decision about their commitment to service. As outlined above, such a commitment involves a process of retrieving the level of spiritual development in a previous lifetime, consolidating that level of initiation in this incarnation, carrying out of this lifetime's mission of service, and moving on to the next higher level of initiation. For example, if the lightbearer had achieved the level of the Second Initiation in a previous lifetime, he or she must regain that level and through further service, can conceivably reach the Third or even Fourth within this lifetime.[31]

During sleep hours, lightbearers continue to meet on the upper levels of the astral plane and actively work together as a group of world servers, preparing for the events that lie ahead. The contradiction between life during sleep and waking hours is what causes the uneasiness and drive to awaken to one's mission, for it is on the conscious level that lightbearers must come to a decision about service to the Spiritual Hierarchy. Once this contradiction is resolved and sleep hour activities blend harmoniously with those of the conscious hours, a sense of peace will reign within.

---

[31] Ascensionists who promise initiating disciples beyond the fourth level are grossly misrepresenting the Path of Initiation.

Life's Demands

During waking hours, too many potential lightbearers are overwhelmed by the details and problems of their earthly lives. Family problems and obligations; unsympathetic spouses; ease and comfort in the material life or, conversely, hardships caused by lack of funds; basic selfishness learned in this incarnation; power ambitions -- all contribute to a range of excuses that prevent many from responding to the urgings of their Higher Selves.

At the same time, the Dark Forces on the astral plane have aimed their attention at these luminaries as they make their way through the blind maze of their present incarnations, tricking and misleading them along the way so that in many cases, some have resorted to drugs or alcoholism, chosen impossible marriage situations, and picked up early illnesses.

The temptations of power and authority have also waylaid many who entered government or corporate fields. Some lightbearers have taken their careers too seriously and have been seized by the *maya* of their profession or position in society. Others know deep down that they are lightbearers but cannot quite let go of the easy life they have achieved. These spiritual dabblers and dilettantes find that requirements for commitment often interrupt human plans.

Even great spiritual luminaries have been sidetracked by psychological problems. Some who have generated large followings borne of the guru-student relationship have been derailed from their path. So dark and confusing have been these times that many lightbearers have lost contact with their original mission. There are thus many lightbearers who have yet to commit to the divine service they promised to fulfill at this point in time, even though they are conscious that something is awakening within them.

Taking into consideration that only one in ten incarnated lightbearers is likely to awaken to fulfill a mission, and most of those will only pay lip service to wanting to serve, the Masters of Wisdom are all-too aware that once incarnated, the memory veil can blind the personality. The Master El Morya describes His experience:

> Since Our introduction to 'society,' We have been subjected to these 'invitations' which would be laughable if so much did not hinge upon them.
>
> The first timid overtures to Us from the 'boldest' spiritual pioneers went something like this . . .'I say! Are you there? Well, if you are, please come in . . . but my world is in perfect systematic running order. *Please don't disturb anything . . . .* It would be 'jolly' if you would stay awhile and *tell me all about myself!'*
>
> Now, on the face of it, We cannot even think of a person without disturbing the rhythm of their worlds, let alone stepping over the threshold into actual association with them; so the door is closed before We can even acknowledge the invitation, if you can call it such!
>
> On the rare occasions when We were permitted to answer and enter the world of the lightbearer, of course *things began to happen.* The living battery of Our energies, no matter how they are muted, energizes everything it touches. Thus when We enter the consciousness, the re-arrangement of the world of the student begins. It is as uncomfortable as all house-moving, renovations and improvements always are to the self, which

enjoys stagnation. Then—the REACTION! Disappointment in the Guests, and usually 'forcible eviction' and thus closes the 'sweet association' between man and his Masters![32]

Thus, as the crises in the world mount, a crisis commitment within the ranks of the lightbearers brews.

Meditation Problems

Meditation is the best way to achieve contact with one's soul. Many dabble with meditation but cannot concentrate or persevere long enough to make any noticeable progress. Many lightbearers struggle with the simplest methods, unable to concentrate or visualise as the mind swirls with life's problems and conflicts. Restlessness pervades, momentary emotional upheavals interrupt, and any practice of regular meditation soon gives way to the other demands of life.

The Master Djwal Khul informs us that a good education trains the mind to concentrate. The scientist, politician, doctor, lawyer, business person — those in any field of endeavour requiring concentration – would tend to succeed better at meditation rather than the untrained mind.

Concentration and visualisation come out of discipline and just plain hard work and willpower. There is no shortcut. Control of the mind's wanderings is the sole task of its owner. Achieving mental control is what separates the useful lightbearer from the spiritual dabbler or dilettante.

---

[32] Printz, Thomas (alias Master Morya), *The First Ray*, Bridge to Freedom, AMTF, pp. 24-25.

Isolation and Fear

Lightbearers are scattered across the earth, participating in all sectors of human society in all countries and cultures. It is unlikely that they are gathered in large concentrations in one particular area. Since there is no church or formal organisation from which they can seek company, their awakening may exacerbate the sense of fear and isolation they, different from birth, may have felt throughout this incarnation. Nevertheless, they must learn to stand on their own and in relative isolation until the day they join other lightbearers. As beacons of the Hierarchy's light in their respective geographical areas, they must learn to be strong, independent workers for the Spiritual Hierarchy, often without monetary remuneration.[33]

Countervailing Astral Influences

Most damaging to the Hierarchy's lightbearer strategy has been the Dark Forces' counter-strategy, designed to block the lightbearer's awakening. The Dark Forces utilize the astral plane to create voices posing as Masters (and even God!) to mislead the lightbearers. Many lightbearers have awakened only to be drawn to follow the voices streaming into their, or others', consciousness from Dark Forces-inspired astral entities instead of their souls. These astral voices, so

---

[33] At the behest of the Master Sanctus Germanus the website www.sanctusgermanus.net was created to serve as a rallying point for lightbearers around the world. One of its purposes is to inform the geographically isolated lightbearer that he or she is not alone and that a wide network of lightbearers is forming.

subtle at times that they resemble one's own thoughts, have misguided many lightbearers into following tantalizing theories of, for example, rapid ascension and DNA activations to reach enlightenment rather than following the nitty gritty of understanding their mission within the Divine Plan. Some of the Hierarchy's most advanced lightbearers have fallen prey to these Dark influences, and once under the Dark regime, they are most often crippled mentally or rendered ineffective for future work with the true Spiritual Hierarchy.

A multitude of Masters and their initiates on the spiritual plane work tirelessly to maintain mental contact with lightbearers in order to guide and remind them of what they had promised to do. Yet many lightbearers ignore these urgings, convincing themselves that other astral voices, which tell them what they want to hear and make them feel good are their legitimate guides.

But despite the critical situation with committed lightbearers, the Spiritual Hierarchy will not compromise on the quality of a lightbearer's commitment.

Commitment Required

The Spiritual Hierarchy holds the candle of hope that most lightbearers will realize their promised mission. If they do not, then the burden will fall on the committed.

First and foremost, the lightbearer must gain a clear vision of his or her role as etched in the soul. Only deep meditation and a sincere intent can bring this role to the conscious mind. Those who wait to be told what to do will wait forever.

Second, the mere knee-jerk instinct for physical survival in face of the earth changes will not suffice as commitment. Half-hearted commitment out of fear will not be sufficient for the Spiritual Hierarchy.

Third, commitment is not alternative employment for lightbearers or their spouses. And, no, the Spiritual Hierarchy will not promise lightbearers a salary to carry out their mission! The heart-felt commitment comes without conditions. Most will find that once engaged, remuneration comes naturally.

Fourth, service must be selfless and benefit those outside the lightbearer's immediate family.

Fifth, as implied above, a commitment to service comes with the retrieval process. We emphasize that this process is already underway: the Masters of Wisdom are working full time with lightbearers around the world, be it through the world's principal religions, its regional and local deities, non-affiliated self-realisation, meditation groups, and the like to nudge lightbearers into action.

Sixth, once committed, lightbearers must work diligently to raise the vibrations of their physical vehicles so they can meet the challenges ahead. Purification of the vehicle is very important.

Seventh, the above considerations point the lightbearer to the practice of White Magic, defined here as divine acts that benefit mankind. When lightbearers again begin practicing White Magic, they are firmly on the path in accordance with the Divine Plan.

Consequences of the Commitment Crisis

If lightbearers are slow to awaken or commit to their mission, then the suffering associated with the three crises—economic depression, world war, and earth changes--will know no bounds. The critical period from 2006 to 2012 will determine whether mankind will twist and turn in the winds of suffering or end, as quickly as possible, the Dark Force regime that has gripped humanity since time immemorial. Whether or not the Army of Lightbearers awakens, the unravelling of the Dark Force-dominated financial system and the suffering this will inflict on mankind will continue. When the Dark Forces seize upon this suffering and utilize the masses of unemployed for their barbaric, militaristic aims, more human suffering will ensue.

Without lightbearers' full-time efforts to bring light to such misery, world suffering will drag on. Lightbearers, adequately prepared as White Magicians, can lead actions of compassion in every community to alleviate human suffering. They cannot stop the march of the pralaya, but they can bring each event to a rapid conclusion and shorten the period of human suffering. This is the great gift that the lightbearers can bring to humankind during the pre-2012 period.

Most of all, their most important contribution lies after this period of human turmoil, for it is in their hands that rests the formation of a transitional society during the Period of Reconstruction that will shape the tenor of the New Golden Age decades from now.

The Inner Leadership Structure Behind The Lightbearers

Because lightbearers are dispersed throughout the world, their force as a group appears structure-less and disorganized. However, no human organisation has the capacity to identify and bring thousands, perhaps millions, of dispersed lightbearers together. Instead, behind this loose earthly structure stands a solid, spiritual structure, which is an integral part of the Spiritual Hierarchy that is guiding each lightbearer to play his or her part in the whole plan. The head of this structure is the Master Sanctus Germanus, better known as Sanctus Germanus, the Hierarch of the New Golden Age. Thousands of Masters, the majority of which are unknown to mankind, work on this project. These Masters are behind every lightbearer, and from their vantage point, they are able to gauge the true motivation and commitment of each.

As the various crises come to a head in the coming years and human governments, institutions and organisations begin to crumble, this structure will begin to manifest. The Masters and their initiates are presently drawing their incarnated lightbearers back into this structure, so that in the near future, there will be a seamless hierarchical structure stretching up from the earth plane into the spiritual dimensions above.

As Above So Below

Lightbearers are thus the essential link between the spirit world and the physical, and as they retrace their Path, they will eventually retrieve their ability to move easily between dimensions and maintain clear communications with the Spiritual Hierarchy. This spiritual link will occur in every field of endeavour. With the help of their counterparts in the spiritual world, a chemist lightbearer, for example, may devise a breakthrough formula, a journalist-lightbearer will arrive with new insights to expose the work of the Dark Forces, and a banker-lightbearer might come to see the financial machinations within the industry and propose reforms.

When lightbearers come together in group service, a counterpart group on the spirit plane is formed to aid the whole endeavour. Or one could say that the earthly group comes together because there is a counterpart group on the spiritual plane. The counterpart group is usually comprised of former colleagues and experts in a given field. So in this way, a strong, but unseen, structure backs the lightbearers' activities, if and when they embark on the service mission they have promised to undertake. This arrangement also helps to keep the activity within the purview of the Divine Plan, for if the human group strays from its mission, members will sense an inner dissatisfaction until they make the effort to realign themselves.

Many lightbearers will be guided to lead the way to the Spiritual Regions well ahead of the most damaging catastrophes. With them go patterns of governance and structures of social organisation known to their counterparts on the etheric plane. These etheric counterparts work with the highest cosmic principles upon which to build a new transitional society; the combination of "ground level" lightbearer groups and their etheric counterparts working together in the Spiritual Regions will give humanity a second opportunity to right the course of humanity's evolution.

Formation of a World Council of Adepts

The Spiritual Hierarchy sends its avatars and Masters onto the earth plane to guide and counsel mankind during periods of turmoil. The Masters of Wisdom, for the most part, work telepathically through their incarnated lightbearers on the earth plane. Yet from time to time they, themselves, will assume astral or etheric bodies to make a visible appearance on earth. Others work more constantly and in secret on the earth plane on all continents. For instance, some Masters are known to attend important political and economic summit meetings disguised as summit participants. They are known to contact discouraged lightbearers "in the flesh" to encourage them. They are also known to overshadow lightbearers and speak through them.

In the coming years, a Council of Adepts will form quietly on the earth plane. This council will be comprised of adepts of the Spiritual Hierarchy who occupy key positions in all fields of endeavour. It is not clear at this point if the Masters will also be members of this Council. For obvious reasons, this Council will remain behind the scenes and operate in secret until conditions on the earth change.

When the Council comes together, it will constitute the guiding light for the world of lightbearers. In each safe area, members of the Council of Adepts will organize a structure based on cosmic principles that will serve and organize the incoming lightbearers. Their first major task is to set up an organisation that can receive displaced persons making their way to the Spiritual Regions from disaster areas.

Leadership Role of the Committed Lightbearer

Let us now concentrate on those lightbearers who have committed themselves to the work of the Spiritual Hierarchy.

The truly committed lightbearer has undertaken to work in a minefield. During the pre-2012 period, the lightbearer's main task is to alleviate human suffering caused by economic depression, war, and initial earth changes. Working against great odds, the lightbearer must regain his or her ability as a White Magician to counter the negative effects of the departing Dark Forces. Humanity is at the point today where only suffering can cause it to open its eyes, and the lightbearer must stand ready and available to help, not as an average person but as a White Magician.

Service in the midst of the major crises will try the lightbearer, and without proper resolve, some may decide to abandon their mission. Those who *choose* to continue their life journey into the New Golden Age must start making the necessary adjustments now. We emphasize that living through the upheavals in the next few decades requires a conscious decision to serve. Lightbearers, who feel their ongoing life commitments are more important and decide to make no change in their lives, will continue to live as much out of harm's way as possible without fulfilling their commitment. Only the Lords of Karma can decide how this non-action will be rebalanced. There is no right or wrong in this choice.

The Spiritual Hierarchy makes no concessions on the quality of the lightbearer's commitment, for was it not the lightbearer who volunteered for the task? Was it not the lightbearer who defined his or her role and contribution according to the Divine Plan?

What lies ahead is not for the weak-minded and spiritual dabblers. At heart must be a complete commitment to carry out one's mission, no matter how menial or difficult it may be. A clear knowledge of one's soul mission borne out of meditation will provide the drive and fortitude the lightbearer needs to follow the path to the Spiritual Regions, deal with huge displacements of the population and eventually participate in the reconstruction of a transitional society that will serve as a model for the New Golden Age.

Opportunities for Co-operation between Lightbearers

In the previous chapter we discussed briefly how the Great Floods will inundate the coastal and low-lying areas of the world. Many of the world's main cities along the coasts will be destroyed causing a toll of life beyond anything we can imagine. At the same time, higher elevation urban centres and the regions surrounding these centres will remain intact.

There are a host of cooperative actions that can be undertaken, following the sequence of the three crises we cited above: the economic depression, the coming war, and the eventual population evacuation caused by the Great Floods. Knowing this sequence, lightbearers can plan well before each of these crises hits.

White Magic: The Basis of ALL Solutions[34]

Faced with overwhelming conditions, what can lightbearers do? First and foremost, each lightbearer must regain complete control over his or her mind so that he or she controls thought rather than thoughts controlling the mind. See chapter 5 for our suggestions on gaining dominion over the mind.

Second, unlike charity or relief organisations dispensing aid, lightbearers can offer spiritually-inspired but practical solutions to problems that confront them. They can heal suffering as White Magicians, much as the Master Jesus did. People in need will seek out the lightbearer to perform such services as telepathic spiritual healing,[35] which can be applied to any dire circumstance, be it the need for food to healing diseases. Sound telepathic healing can help individuals and groups in times of need.

At the start, lightbearers as White Magicians must be very discreet in helping people, for most will not understand White Magic. Spiritual guides and the Masters will direct people in need to lightbearers, or lightbearers will be placed in situations where silent meditation and the invocation of White Magic may be the only solution. Many "miracles" will occur from lightbearers' actions, and by their works, other spiritually–inclined people will gather around them for solace and comfort. The crises, in other words, present enormous opportunities for service and compassion.

---

[34] See Bailey, Alice A., *A Treatise on White Magic.*
[35] The Sanctus Germanus Foundation is training telepathic healers who will train lightbearers to practice telepathic healing.

Highland-Lowland Cooperation Pattern

Lightbearers located in areas which will most likely be flooded should follow the promptings of their spiritual guides to inform their communities and to begin planning to move to higher elevations. Those already located in the higher elevation centres have been placed there to prepare for the influx of displaced lowland populations. A natural cooperation between highland and lowland lightbearers thus will exist to meet this eventual crisis. Lightbearers in both the safe and endangered areas in a particular region should begin to work together to plan how they will cope with the crises ahead.

Economic Depression: Opportunities for Lightbearers

A key role among lightbearers during this period will be to help alleviate suffering caused by a worldwide economic depression. Millions will be unemployed, paper money will lose its value, families will be forced out into the streets and many ordinary people will be reduced to begging on the streets. Walking through the streets and seeing such misery, lightbearers will be called upon for mental and spiritual healing not only of the general situation but of individuals.

Signs of Local Economic Stress

The worldwide economic depression is expected to hit bottom in late 2007. From that point, there will be no recovery for years to come, and the world in general will revert to basic living. At first the signs will not be so apparent, but as the years drag on, the stress will become more overt.

Lightbearers should not rely on the media and governments for any confirmation as they will be in denial. Instead, lightbearers should look in their immediate communities for the following signs:

- Higher than usual unemployment
- "For Sale" signs in front of houses as the worldwide real estate bubble pops
- Bankruptcies of stores and businesses on the main commercial thoroughfares, empty and boarded up store-fronts
- Local bank failures and runs on the bank
- Increasing number of families on welfare
- More ordinary people begging on the streets
- Greater number of homeless families crowding into charitable organisations
- More and more people resorting to exchanging services rather than paying cash
- Resurrection of depression-style soup kitchens.
- Increase in crime
- Harsher local police tactics
- Militarization of the population: more people in uniform

On the national and international levels, the US dollar, the world's reserve currency, will tank and continue to slide in value until it is worth almost zero.

The Euro will seem stronger for a short time, but will also decline as confidence in any paper fiat money wanes. The worldwide price of gold will easily shoot pass US$1000.00 per ounce and continue upward without any restraint.

All these signs spell a hyper-inflationary situation that will empty every wallet and pocketbook. People will be forced to pay for goods and services with silver or gold or carry wheelbarrows of worthless paper money to purchase their daily needs. This situation has already happened in many countries — Argentina, the Congo, Guinea, Vietnam, Albania and Russia are recent examples of how overnight poverty can become a reality.

The economic depression brings many opportunities for highland/lowland cooperation among lightbearers. It will result in an initial displacement of people as they are dispossessed of their material belongings and homes and search for employment. More and more personal bankruptcies will force people to move from urban areas to the countryside. This early "economic" shift of populations should preferably take place from the lowlands to the highlands.

Lightbearers should use whatever means at their disposal to encourage people to move to higher elevations. Because they are able to see into the future, they should inform the general populace of what is likely to happen. They can speak to disaster relief agencies and charitable organisations in their area to adopt policies. Information is powerful, but it is still up to the individual to take this information to heart and act on it.

Lightbearers already located at higher elevation destinations can prepare local authorities for an influx of the displaced. The potential for conflict between the incoming populations and the residents of the highland areas is great, and lightbearers can play a role in receiving their fellow brothers and sisters in these areas. This may be a touchy situation requiring much diplomacy, as the first reaction of such communities will be to bar newcomers. The more prepared for this eventuality, the better.

The displaced will need food, shelter, clothing, and fresh water. Many of the existing disaster relief organisations have already adopted procedures to help local residents cope with disaster, but are they prepared for mass population movements and the social chaos that follows? They will not be able to turn to crippled national governments for help. The magnitude of such population displacements will overwhelm authorities, so lightbearers must take a lead role in organizing groups to handle this. Forewarned is forearmed.

Cooperative efforts among lightbearers as well as existing groups could include the following:

- Organizing gardens on vacant lands to provide food
- Using abandoned buildings in the elevated areas to house displaced persons
- Identifying fresh water sources
- Collecting used clothing for use in the future

- Locate and gain access to arenas, community halls, recreation halls, school gymnasiums, etc. to host the homeless and itinerants
- Locate cafeterias in all of the facilities that can be used as basic soup kitchens, etc.
- Talk to churches to house the homeless

As the economic shift of the populations continues, lightbearers in lowland areas should seriously consider moving to higher ground in preparation for the floods. If early flooding occurs where lightbearers are located, this should serve as a concrete signal that a move to higher ground is required. Lightbearers must reach this decision by themselves and muster the resources to make the move. There will be no one to tell them what to do and on arrival at higher ground there will be no reception committee to welcome them. They must make the tough decision to uproot their lives and make the move on their own initiative, based on guidance from their spiritual guides. This may mean giving up their homes and detaching from all possessions that will not help them in this phase of their mission. This requires a quantum leap of faith and foreknowledge.

All lightbearers will need a firm and definite plan of where to go before disaster hits. They should investigate possible destinations near the Spiritual Regions. Like many others already in place in those areas, lightbearers should either move or make definite plans to move - the earlier, the better.

Cooperative Efforts during the War: Time to Move

When world war breaks out and the draft is reinstated in the US and other countries, it will be time for lightbearers to move to their chosen Spiritual Regions. There should be no doubt at this point that the sequence of prophecies outlined in Volume 1 of *The Sanctus Germanus Prophecies* by the Spiritual Hierarchy is taking place. All the seeds have been sown for World War III.

The Council of Adepts will begin to emerge and guide lightbearers in the nascent Spiritual Regions. Planning ahead, they will organize the reception of the displaced. The march of events will not pause for the reluctant Lightbearer. Those in the know will labour persistently and consequently receive the highest support from the Spiritual Hierarchy. They will alleviate suffering to the best of their abilities and in this way more survivors will join their ranks as events unfold.

By 2010, spiritual guides will prompt many lightbearers to move to one of the Spiritual Regions. Lightbearers will filter into these areas by their own accord and re-group both in the cities and rural areas of these regions. As more earth changes dominate the news, they will be reassured that they have made the right move.

The earlier (i.e. 2007 onward) this transmigration takes place the better. In many parts of the world, e.g. North and South America, Asia, Europe and the Indian sub-continent this movement of lightbearers has already started. Small communities have set up in the mountain areas of North and South America. In the

Himalayan foothills, a substantial Buddhist infrastructure is in place and certain lamas are keenly aware of the coming earth changes. Their system of mutual aid is well known.

Wartime Work of the Lightbearers

War pits mankind against itself. All war is civil war, brothers and sisters against their own. War is rooted in greed and selfishness, not in ideology or religion. There are no wrong or right sides. Both sides of war are the tools of the Dark Forces, pitted against one another so that the Dark Forces can satisfy their greed for money. So every battle is essentially one of Light versus Darkness.

War is the greater manifestation of the battle raging in each one of us on the astral plane. The Dark Forces can manipulate billions of inner conflicts into warring nations. This is easily done through propaganda sent through the media to pound this point of view into the minds of people and agitate their emotions.

A world society suffering in the midst of an economic depression makes excellent fodder for warmongers. World War II rose out of the ashes of the 1929 Depression. Governments will fail to quell social chaos resulting from the depression, and the military, under the direct control of the Dark Forces, will take over to maintain law and order. This is the institutionalization of repression, as the militarization of the civilian population will be presented as the only solution to economic chaos; we can see this happening now. Millions of men and women will be mobilized into the military to conduct war.

The Dark Forces are fully aware that this is the last battle with the Light Forces. Knowing that defeat is inevitable, the Dark Forces will resort to the most drastic and spectacular measures to sow fear and terrify mankind. These include using nuclear weapons. There will be no restraints this time, and for this reason, many souls will choose to exit earth voluntarily rather than live under nuclear fallout, military repression and war. Memories of military repression as seen in the post-World War II Stalinist era still remain fresh. This time, it could be worse.

Lightbearers cannot prevent this war, as mobilization for it started at least a decade ago and continues. Yet the light they bear on the war will bring it to a speedier end. Humanity must undergo this karmic balancing, for is it not responsible for permitting the rise and power of the Dark Forces? Did it not acquiesce to their temptations of a materialistic life and allow itself to be lulled into a stupor? Karmic rebalancing vis à vis the Dark Forces is a process humanity cannot escape.

War brings out the worst in mankind. Lightbearers can bring out the best. The horrors of war ironically lead mankind back to its essence, its soul, which remains above the fray and always in a state of purity. No thinking person can resist the call of the soul to turn inward when faced with the carnage of war. Even the hardest individual will sink to his knees when faced with or threatened by such atrocities.

The coming world war presents a golden opportunity for the lightbearer to come to the fore and demonstrate the opposite of war. The Spiritual Hierarchy works through its Light Forces on the earth plane, and when the lightbearers join hands to draw down Truth and Light upon the *maya* of war, they can shorten the duration of human suffering and foil the efforts of the Dark Forces.

Lightbearers can use all means to educate the public about the war - who the warring parties truly are and what the war truly is about i.e. greed. They may choose to actively resist participation in the war. Many lightbearers between the ages of 18 and 42 could be drafted into the military against their will. They can use legal methods such as conscientious objection to perform alternative service or remove themselves from the reach of conscription. Nothing can justify this war, as it is the pure invention of the Dark Forces. Do not be fooled by the nationalistic or patriotic jingoism, which is used to mislead people and stir them into aggression.

These actions create the proper invocation for the externalisation of the Hierarchy. Lightbearers, who have responded to their souls' call and taken action, will work with the Spiritual Hierarchy to counter the effects of war. Those who do not want to wage war can call upon the Spiritual Hierarchy to provide their escape avenue.

More inter-dimensional forces have been called up to reinforce the lagging earthly effort, making the meaning of the externalization of the Hierarchy more relevant than ever. With the necessary channels open to the power and light of the Hierarchy, light can shine down on every battle and render the Dark Forces' reign of terror null and void. Cosmic law dictates that White Magic always wins over black, and the more the forces of White Magic come together on all dimensions, the greater the force of good and the shorter the reign of terror of the Dark Forces.

Early Warnings of Earth Changes to Come

As the economic depression and world war grip the world, signs of earth changes will abound. Global warming will cause the seas and other water bodies to inch up while periodic storms, flash floods, prolonged heavy rains, hurricanes and freak storms increase their steady thrusts on all areas. Governments will disseminate contradictory climatic information to convince flood victims that minor, cyclic freak weather patterns are to blame. Lightbearers should interpret these signs as a compelling reason to move to areas close to the Spiritual Regions ahead of the mass displacements. Many will be forced to move, but many will foolishly return to the flooded areas to rebuild.

The general population in the lowland areas will balk at the need to move and wait until it is too late. All lightbearers can do is to inform. As is usually the case, the majority will wait to the very last minute, and a mass, uncoordinated rush to the elevated regions will ensue.

Conclusion

The clock is ticking, and as every year passes, earth changes will increase in frequency and intensity. As part of the Spiritual Hierarchy's strategy, the lightbearers are set to play the same role Noah did with his ark in the previous diluvium, although in not such a folkloric way. They are the preservers of mankind's knowledge and civilisation, which they will carry into the post-diluvium transitional society that shapes the Golden Era.   There is still hope that the Light Forces on earth will awaken to their mission and take action in the numbers that were foreseen by the Divine Plan.

CHAPTER 5

Achieving Dominion over the Events

"Wise is he who takes the staff in hand, and walks the Way himself, with eyes open, heart attuned to the Spirit's voice, and keeping his own watch, lingers not in the false security of another's achievement, but as a fellow-traveller, blesses him, but makes of the goal of his experiences dependent on his endeavours . . .for such attain the victory."[36] *El Morya*

In the foreword to this book the Master Sanctus Germanus makes it clear that remaining on earth during the pralaya is a matter of choice. If you do not face this situation here on earth, you will eventually face it elsewhere. And from an eternal perspective, there is really no rush. If you wish to know more about what commitment entails, please read on. Otherwise, you may skip this chapter and go on to the next.

When the Spiritual Hierarchy drew up plans for this period, you were among the most enthusiastic souls chosen by the Karmic Board out of the thousands or perhaps millions who volunteered. However, once

---

[36] Printz, Thomas, op. cit. p. 151

in the thick *maya* of the earth plane, your enthusiasm dampened, and the goals of your incarnation became obscured.

For some, the material benefits of today's civilisation have eluded them, forcing them to battle for the necessities of daily life and in the process, veering them off course. Many harbour sub-conscious guilt and disdain for money, which the Dark Forces have fostered through the traditional religions and the New Age Movement. As a consequence, money energy has eluded them, perpetuating a deprived state and ongoing resentment at society or God for making things so difficult. For others, position and money have led to comfortable and "successful" lifestyles that override any deep commitment to the spiritual quest. Spiritual dilettantes gather on cruise ships, at tropical spas and hideaways, follow their gurus from place to place or retire to mountain retreats to partake in "feel good" programs generated by the pseudo-spiritual movement. Both extremes have created different brands of self-centeredness that have stymied the implementation of the Divine Plan.

Moreover, the Dark Forces have targeted the lightbearers and tricked many of them into a genre of pseudo-spirituality that gives lip service to group action while at the same time spawning personality quirks that result in splintering group efforts. All spiritual groups are targeted to keep these groups from coming together.

Today, many lightbearers just like you "feel" something is amiss, but most would rather discount the warning storms and wars as yet another minor cycle. Rather than risk too much disruption in their lives, most would prefer to remain oblivious to or refuse to acknowledge that major changes are about to occur. So the formation of the "troops" for this final battle has been less than satisfactory as the commitment of the lightbearer to resist or battle the Dark Forces' offensive falters. The numbers of Light Forces the Spiritual Hierarchy expected have not materialized and if this situation persists, the suffering humanity must bear will be prolonged.

The Spiritual Hierarchy recently conceded that its strategy to build an Army of Lightbearers on earth may be in jeopardy. But hope springs eternal. Out of all those volunteers who did incarnate, the Spiritual Hierarchy realistically estimated they could count on one in ten (1:10) to fulfill their mission. However, whether or not the number of committed lightbearers is even smaller than one-tenth, the work and preparation will continue. The economic, financial and geological changes are on schedule and will not wait for people to make up their minds.

Despite this seemingly unfortunate situation, a core of hardy lightbearers has emerged out of the *maya*, who, with balanced mental and astral bodies, has thrown off the "feel good" quest and seriously committed itself to the Divine Plan. They know that the fleeting seconds of "feel-good" come only when they cast off an emotional or physical shackle that allows them to advance further along the thorny Path of Initiation to fulfill their mission. Every "feel good" moment is preceded by long periods of struggle, both physical and emotional.

These few and hardy will bear the burden as events unfold and will receive the full backing of the

Spiritual Hierarchy and the Master Sanctus Germanus. So even as the agitation on the astral plane ramps up further and the Dark Forces target the "one-tenth", they will find battle-hardened troops covered with mystic armour.

The great hope remains that the catastrophes will awaken reluctant and hesitant lightbearers to their true purpose. The door always remains open. But if you are that one-tenth in incarnation, much preparatory work lies ahead in the relatively short time before the looming catastrophes.

Retrieval of Your Previous Spiritual Level

We mentioned above that you volunteered to incarnate even though most of you had achieved a high level of spiritual development that took you out of the wheel of incarnations. You thus understood and accepted the fact that by coming back this lifetime, you would build up more good and bad karma. Most of you chose to work off your residual karma early in this lifetime in order that the second half of your lifetime could be spent doing the good works associated with your awakening.

Gaining Spiritual Confidence

When you embark on your journey of retrieval, the Path will not be as straightforward as you expect. Sometimes you will experience elation at the discovery of a spiritual truth, yet there will be times when you feel you are butting against a stonewall, making no progress at all. You may also encounter false prophets or incompetent psychics and mediums who may mislead you. You may join spiritual groups that may be so fraught with conflict and disagreements that you may wonder if spirit is love.

The cryptic language in some of the occult literature may intimidate you or even discourage you completely as you read pages and pages before you seize one idea. Or you may discover that easier spiritual pabulum dished out by so many spiritual teachers makes you feel good for the moment but lets you down in the long run. In desperation, you may throw yourself at the feet of a guru or mentor only to find that he or she does not deserve your attention.

Embarking on a spiritual "career" will necessarily change your life radically. Your old friends and family may shy away from you, and you may find yourself surrounded by an entirely new circle of friends, some confused and flaky, others understanding and sympathetic. You may even travel great distances in search of the truth, only to return empty-handed.

All these ups and downs may cause you to lose confidence in your ability to grasp the spiritual side of life. This is perfectly normal. Nevertheless, you are advised to persist, for you are being put through numerous tests—the initial obstacle course—that will help transform you into a tried and true lightbearer. Some will never regain their confidence and give up. Those who pursue and persist in their quest will eventually find the answers, and that is the **PROMISE** of this whole process. There is indeed a treasure at the end of the rainbow. So the key to this journey is *persistence*.

Looking Inward for Answers

Although the Masters of the Spiritual Hierarchy stand ready to pour their aid and guidance upon committed lightbearers, they also require that you look inward first for answers. Your Higher Self, Causal Body or the I AM knows your plan and communicates freely with the Masters without the misleading interference of astral entities. Therefore, the reconnection with your inner prelate, your Higher Self, is essential to joining the Army of Light.

Today, we are bombarded with false information coming from the media as well as from the astral plane in a form pretending to be own thoughts. You cannot count on your government or any other outside organisation to guide or help you when disaster hits. The fact that the national governments, charitable organisations, even disaster relief agencies are unaware of or play down the coming changes should indicate that everyone is woefully unprepared, despite the multitude of warnings the Masters of the Spiritual Hierarchy have communicated to humanity. Added to this general unpreparedness is the constant stream of contradictory information streaming into your thought processes from astral entities.

Yet, deep within each one of us, in our inner self, the I AM, we can access all the correct information about what is to come as well as take part in a vast spiritual organizational structure that IS prepared to guide us to safety so we can pursue our mission during this critical period. You, alone, must rely on yourself because access to this spiritual structure is through your inner world.

1. Master the In-Breath Meditation Method

The Spiritual Hierarchy strongly recommends that lightbearers adopt the In-Breath Meditation Method to reconnect with their Higher Selves. This method is based on the original precepts of Raja Yoga and uses the control of and focus on breathing to drive your conscious self into your inner world and thus contact with your Higher Self.

There are many ways to meditate. Some are valid and others are not. Guided meditations are limited in what they can do for individual responsibility, even if the intent is good. Meditating is, first and foremost, **your** responsibility, and when this responsibility is met and mastered, the next step is group meditation, not the other way around. A group of people where each one has mastered their ability to meditate can become a powerful force for light. However, a group where you cede to a leader can amount to mental manipulation.

The In-Breath Meditation Method suggested below puts the entire responsibility of meditation on you, as it should be. It relies on the control of your breathing and your ability to concentrate and direct your thinking. It is ultimately you who takes the responsibility for the meditation and its outcome. But the best reward that comes from this meditation is the pilgrimage you make to your Higher Self, that prelate who resides within you. And the more you practice this method, the more you align yourself to your Higher Self and the information it seeks to convey to you.

This method is so simple that it is difficult. There are times you will feel as though you are getting nowhere, but do not give up. Rein in your thoughts, concentrate, and keep pursuing.

In-Breath Meditation Method for Profound Spiritual Growth and Soul Contact

Meditation when properly understood is the stilling of the physical body, generally in a position where the spine is straight and erect, sitting up, not lying down.

You should define a place of meditation that is fairly comfortable as to temperature and where you are likely not to be disturbed by others. An ambiance or atmosphere of the spirit should be cultivated around it if possible.

When you sit to meditate, you must come to feel that you are about to have a conversation with your God, your Higher Self, and nothing less. You should approach meditation as you approach the altar of invocation--with humility, awe, respect, great love and gratitude.

With the proper attitude, approach, and place, we suggest the following meditation procedure:

1. Sit in a comfortable posture with you spine straight and erect. You may sit in the traditional yogi's meditation position or straight up in a comfortable chair.

2. Invoke the Violet Flame of Protection

3. Begin to breathe deeply and honour the breath that is yours to draw in and to exhale. And with each breath, realize that you are drawing in pure life and light.

4. As you breath deeply, initially focus your attention in the head area, the top of the head in particular. Become aware of your own aura.

5. Then become aware of and focus on the entire length of the spine, as you remain conscious of the rhythm of your breath. Breathe in, breathe out.

6. Now, release the attention on the breathing and let it continue at the proper pace by itself.

7. Focus all your attention on the entire length of the spinal column and hold the attention there. Visualize the length of the spine as a tube of pure white light.

8. See the tube of light as a doorway that is slightly ajar. On the other side of the doorway is much light. The doorway, the lit spinal column, is now a lovely dimensional doorway into your inner space.

9. You begin to have the desire to go into it, for it is indeed a doorway. It is a dimensional opening in the physical body. You seek to go in it. You have the will to go in, and in, and in. You must will yourself to go in, not unlike one paddling a canoe upstream against the current and not unlike the salmon that doggedly keep swimming upstream against the current that keeps beating them back. But they don't stop. Use your will to go in, in, in.

10. As you meditate in this way, you will hit at some point, a landmark, so to speak. You'll know what it is by the sheer experience of it. If you think you cannot go any deeper, you should keep trying until you cannot go any more. At this point, stop and simply enjoy the inner surroundings.

11. Seek to become aware of the inner atmosphere as the breath continues to inhale and exhale at its own steady pace.

12. Seek to know yourself as you are, beyond thoughts, feelings, sensations and certainly physical bodies. Every session will be a new adventure.

13. Seek to know that part of you that has never changed and shall never change, the part of you that is eternal. Seek to feel your own endlessness.

This may seem like a very cursory and basic approach to meditation but we assure you that if properly followed, it will lead you to inner breakthroughs of the type that most people so much want to experience but are so unaware of how to.

2. Reconnect with Your Master

If you are not yet aware of the Master you are working under, you can use the In-Breath Meditation Method to get this information. The meditation will put you in contact with your Higher Self whom you can ask to guide you to the Master in charge of your awakening. Be assured, however, that once you are ready to re-establish contact, your Master will in one way or another make that contact clear to you.

In the beginning the answers come back to your conscious mind in the form of strong intuitions, not voices. If you hear voices, you may be hearing unreliable astral entities that are trying to worm their way into your communication. In this case, strive deeper into your meditation. This is the safest way to get the correct information, for during these times of extreme astral plane excitement, hordes of astral entities would love to become your "master" and lead you off track. Many voices claiming to be Masters will intervene. They will speak in the language of spirituality and subtly lead you astray.

Study the Ancient Wisdom as it has been laid out for westerners over the past 150 years. The Theosophical Society's wealth of writings, the I AM Discourses by Sanctus Germanus, the prolific instructions by the Master Djwal Khul through his amanuensis Alice A. Bailey, the Bridge to Freedom discourses from the Brotherhood through Geraldine Innocenti, the early works of the Summit Lighthouse movement and finally the website (www.sanctusgermanus.net) of the Sanctus Germanus Foundation, all represent the trail of information on the Ancient Wisdom that the Spiritual Hierarchy has meticulously laid out for you to study.

This body of works represents an enormous resource of spiritual information that the Spiritual Hierarchy has put forth for lightbearers in order that they reclaim their ability to discriminate between what is real and the unreal. The language and depth of this body of knowledge will help you distinguish between the false voices from the astral plane and the thought-forms your Master transmits to you.

Even if you are reminded of just a fraction of the revealed Ancient Wisdom, you will know enough to repulse astral influences and discriminate between your true intuitions and chatty voices offering advice of all sorts.[37] These entities are for the most part astral shells without any inherent intelligence and speak like puppets, so you can very quickly gain more knowledge than they to distinguish right from wrong.

In reality, being able to discriminate between voices is no different from normal human interactions on earth. Exercise the same discrimination when walking through a crowded marketplace full of hawkers selling their wares. You will recognize a fast-talking sales pitch from the truth, while others will fall for it. Ultimately, you must decide to whom you will listen, and if you are confused by the cacophony of astral voices, seek refuge in the In-Breath Meditation and sink yourself into the inner world. There, your Higher Self will always tell you the truth.

3. Probationary Period: Follow the Guidance of Your Master

After you have reconnected with your Master, you will then undergo yet another probationary period,

---

[37] Some of their advice is useful in the beginning so that they can gain your confidence, but they will inevitably lead you off the path to their own dark agenda.

because the Spiritual Hierarchy knows too well that there are pitfalls all along the Path that can trip the most advanced initiate.

When you first trod the probationary path many lifetimes ago, it may have taken your soul several incarnations to graduate. This time, however, you will unconsciously retread the probationary path, but in quick time, perhaps in months or a couple years. This is why we call this process a retrieval. You will be *reminded* more than taught anew.

During the probationary period the Master wants to see if the desire to serve is a result of a momentary life crisis or motivated by a genuine soul desire to serve. If you give up during this period, you are then put under the care of your spiritual guides who will work with you further to retrieve your soul motivation for service, if you so desire.

If you pursue, you will come under the special scrutiny and care of your Master. You have asked for assistance and must thus undergo more stringent discipline. You learn to master power over all substance, vibration and form. You accept to cleanse all latent vice and strengthen the latent virtue. From then on, all your activities reflect upon the Master, and Master's desire becomes your "heart desire". You must employ your talents and capacities in this service.

The Master will constantly test you by putting you through experiences that will develop and mature the body vehicle until it masters a more superior degree of energy control, not only on the earth plane, but on the other inner planes as well. The Master can access your inner bodies to reinforce weaknesses for the most protection or that part of the seven-body vehicle that is destined to take the hardest knocks. The Master will concentrate on that inner body which you will use most in carrying out your mission. The aim is to develop and mature the body vehicle for the mission ahead, although it may seem painful and trying to you at times. Better that the Master weave the mystic armour over your Achilles heel than leave it vulnerable to the thrust of evil!

The probationary period may last months or years and depends upon the amount of karma you have accumulated or repaid in this lifetime and upon the amount of discipline you are willing to accept. Some drop out under the pressure of this constant testing, while others will endure and pursue to the end.

The Master will then begin entrusting you with spiritual information. How you choose to use this information requires spiritual discernment and discretion over when to speak and what to withhold from "profane eyes." This is the discipline you must develop. There are experiences which may be spoon-fed to a chosen few and there are many beautiful and delightful experiences that can be told to inspire others. However, you must be on permanent guard against indiscretions born of enthusiasm, love and zeal.

4. The Accepted Lightbearer: Work Together with the Master

Once you prove to be reliable and able to handle information and knowledge with discretion, you will be accepted as an official lightbearer. You and your Master become one in consciousness.

The Master will often ask you to render a service in order to conserve energy, as most Masters are involved with multiple projects. The Master will delegate tasks to you and other trustworthy pupils, according to your particular talents, in order to further a particular cause.

At this stage, the Master may offer you suggestions as to how to hasten your retrieval while at the same time becoming of greater assistance to the work at hand. The Master may convey this message directly to you or through an advanced initiate. The latter becomes the "lifeline " between the Master and other possible students who cannot communicate directly with the Master.

When you pass certain tests, you become the "accepted" lightbearer who will continue on to retrieve your level of Initiation. From thereon, you serve into Adeptship, and finally full mastery.

In conclusion, the reconnection with your Master is of prime importance in order to know your role and place in the Divine Plan that will unfold during this pralaya. When the working relationship is established, both the Higher Self's purpose and the Master's guidance operate in harmony and tandem with each other. This is the ideal partnership that enables you to carry out your mission with success.

5. Learn Discrimination

Once your perceptions open up to the other dimensions, you will be the focus of much astral chatter from the astral plane. Voices posing as your Master will stroke your ego and worm themselves into

your confidence. Here is a passage of advice that the
Master Kuthumi offers:

> *Every life stream on the Path, sooner or later, comes
> to a certain point where he begins to turn to the "still
> small place" within the heart. At first the individual
> begins to rely on intuition, then on inspiration, and,
> later still, upon that conscious contact which precedes
> self-conscious mastery, the attainment of which
> constitutes his divine freedom from all human concepts
> and all human form.*
>
> *This is the most difficult point upon the spiritual
> path and I ask that you come to the place where you
> enter into the heart of the silence--where you commune
> with your own God-self, that you be extremely wise,
> alert and careful of the response that you will receive
> first of all from your own bodies, because you are a
> complex mechanism--a sevenfold being. Now, whereas
> the glory of your electronic body, your Causal Body and
> your Holy Christ self can never lead you astray--your
> lower bodies have voice, consciousness and intelligence
> of their own--and these voices, this consciousness and
> this intelligence within them endeavour often to serve
> its own selfish ends through you.*
>
> *One of the chief requirements for spiritual mastery is
> discrimination. Call to me, if you wish, to my beloved
> Lord Maitreya, or to the great Lord Buddha for that
> discrimination wherein you may recognize the Voice of
> the Silence.*
>
> *Know always that the prompting which builds up the
> personality, that which gives aggrandizement to the
> human Ego, is not the "still small voice" of the
> Presence, but rather the etheric rumblings of your own
> past experiences, the emotional desires of your feeling
> world, or mental concepts and precepts from your past
> lives.*
>
> *Remember if you have sat in the past before many
> teachers who have given forth both truth and fallacy
> and into your mental and emotional bodies and your*

*etheric consciousness have built those concepts, some of them solidified and petrified and lying dormant within them for centuries, as the flame begins to surge through you, these concepts are revivified and come forth, and you must recognize them for what they are-- **not necessarily of the Voice of Truth!***

As you proceed into an understanding of the voice of the silence, know that that which makes you humble, that which makes you loving, that which makes you purer, that which makes you harmonious, is of God. The feelings that stir within your heart that desire to make of this star a planet of light, to relieve the burden of your fellow man, to raise those in pain and distress into understanding and harmony--that is of Light. That which decreases the personality and increases the power of Christ--that is of God![38]

One of the great dangers in dealing with astral entities as if they were divine Masters is that if you let one into your confidence, you virtually open the door to ALL of them. The reason is that the entity who is posing as a Master cannot protect you from others of the same vibrations. In other words, that entity has no superior vibrations over others of the same ilk. So even if you invoke Violet Flame protection from any of the hundreds of Sanctus Germanus' impostors, it would be in vain, since doing so would be detrimental to their own survival!

So learn to discriminate between the impostors and the real through developing your knowledge of the Ancient Wisdom as armour against any impostor or astral shell that may try to trick you. Do not rely on your "feelings" as they can be manipulated astrally but instead listen to your Higher Self and the intuitions it

---

[38] Innocenti, op. cit.

sends to your conscious mind. You can always count on your Higher Self or IAM to convey to you the Truth.

6. Take Responsibility for Your Earthly Self

In all aspects of your earthly life from hereon, take responsibility for yourself. If you are facing emotional crises in your family or workplace, do not spend time blaming others but see them as your responsibility to resolve. Many of you have entered into relationships or marriages that literally beat you into the ground of emotional turmoil. Get used to taking the initiative to either quietly remove yourself from such situations or resolve the problem once and for all. You are not a victim of circumstances but master of them. Part of your training with your Master will strengthen you to rely on the deep inner voice rather than spurious public media.

Take responsibility for your finances. If you are in dire financial shape, look deeply into the cause. You probably got yourself into the financial mess, and you must get yourself out of it. You would be surprised what resources come your way once you take complete responsibility for it and decide to do something about it!

We stress taking responsibility for yourself because this is part of the spiritual development that will prepare you for the crumbling of human institutions we have leaned on for centuries. You have already observed the flooding that has started in certain regions of the world. You have undoubtedly noted that that national and local governments responsible for the peoples' welfare have proven their ineptitude or been overwhelmed by these minor disasters. If they cannot cope with these, how will they face the greater catastrophes ahead? You cannot count on them to help, so prepare yourselves accordingly.

Your local disaster relief agency or Red Cross agencies have published instructions on preparations you might consider in your planning. We would suggest that you make preparations for a longer timeframe than that suggested. If you are living on the coastal areas and low-lying areas near inland water bodies, you should identify a safe, elevated destination and how to get there if you have to evacuate.

The Sanctus Germanus Foundation will post messages from the Spiritual Hierarchy on www.sanctusgermanus.net. These messages should serve to guide and inform you well ahead of the events.

We emphasize again the need to take responsibility for yourself, for the enormity of the earth changes coupled by the financial and economic crises will touch everyone. Mass media and governments are limited in what they can do, so reliance on your wonderful spiritual guides who are only one step away from you is essential. They are working in concert with the Divine Plan, and if you are open and ready to listen, they will guide you.

7. Purify the Body Vehicle

Given the opening of the physical body to etheric faculties in the very near future, we would suggest that you establish a program to purify your body vehicle through regular detoxification or fasting. Both are essential to allow the body to adjust to the accelerated vibrations. A toxic state in the body will collide with these higher vibrations and cause many discomforts.

The need to detoxify is as old as humanity itself; however, the urgency to detoxify is the call of the times. The present knowledge of detoxification is more than adequate. Many of the ancient religions such as Hinduism and Buddhism have developed very effective methods of purification that are still valid for the present circumstances. For instance, the Ayurvedic Panchakarma system of detoxification, the five do's, is a well-established methodology to purge the body of toxins. Even the ancient Christians periodically fasted and detoxified.

You really do not need complicated and expensive herbal detoxification packages. Regular juice fasting is a relatively easy way to purify the body vehicle. Stop eating and drink juice for one or two days per week. Fasting will gradually lead to a change in your diet. As the body is purified, your mind will become sharper and your body will lose the extra pounds, which are but adipose tissue laden with accumulated toxins. The sharper mind will enable you to be more open to telepathic communication with your spiritual guides.

The purer the body vehicle, the lighter foods your body will require. Let the type of body vehicle you are wearing determine your diet. Vegetarianism does not necessarily make you any holier than a non-vegetarian. Many of you have lived past lives as very holy vegetarians and have come back this time in omnivorous bodies. This is because a healthy and hardy body vehicle is what will be needed to withstand both the physical and mental stress in the coming years.

Some of you under the influence of tobacco smoking, excessive consumption of alcohol, or addictive "recreational" drugs must work valiantly to free yourselves by whatever means of these influences. The toxicity pumped into the physical vehicle by these habits can only slow your retrieval process or in most cases completely sabotage your mission.

The Masters will sometimes try to work around these addictions, yet in all known cases, the lightbearer eventually becomes too unreliable and unstable to handle information and carry out important tasks according to the Divine Plan.

8. Purify the Astral Body

Purifying your physical body is only part of the process of purification. The great scourge of modern times is the accumulated store of emotions that one feeds into the astral body. This layer of emotional problems blocks the ready contact that the dense physical body should have with its mental body and the etheric double. All of these hidden emotions are stored in the astral body of an individual.

Higher and finer etheric energies are pouring into earth increasing the frequency within which we must live. They are also substantially cleaning out the astral plane as well as your astral body. So whether we are ready or not, our astral bodies and our emotional bodies are undergoing a cleansing. Those who are not ready will resort to insane behaviour while those who are ready will weather the cleansing.

Understand what is happening when you lose your temper over something insignificant. Understand why others are behaving insanely even to the point of harming their neighbours. In most cases, it is like torture. Some will go insane, others may opt to leave the earth, while the strong, sane and hardy will face up to the emotions that come to the surface and deal with them. This clearing is happening and will continue until all the dross has surfaced and been swept away.

As this process takes hold, you will become very aware that your own upheaval is part of a worldwide process rather than a personal one. It becomes personal when you "take the bull by the horns" and deal with specific exposed emotions. Some long-forgotten emotions that you have suppressed will surface when you least expect it. They may puzzle you, and you may ask yourself why these thoughts are suddenly popping into your consciousness. You must face them. If you need to forgive, do so. If you need to admit you were wrong, do so. If you think a great injustice was done to you and you still harbour resentment, let it go, for you are the only one that gives it life.

Surfacing emotions may even cause unusual aches and pains. Yoga is excellent to handle this release. When the emotions lash out as fear or hatred, you must act as your own psychologist and handle these emotions through meditation or deal with them head-on through decisions to transmute them into the universe. Drop the hatred, forgive and forget.

Today's psychologists are ill-equipped to handle the welling up of these emotions, especially since they do not recognize that a universal filtering is in progress. Prescription drugs only compound the problems. They will try to treat emotional problems in other mechanical and less-than-satisfactory ways. In fact, psychologists, psychiatrists, and the medical profession will admit to being overwhelmed, if not bewildered by the insanity around us today.

Some New Age healing modalities claim to lift these emotional blockages out of a person. Life should be so easy! Energy therapy can help detox and may even help bring emotional problems to the surface, but it is up to you to deal with them. In other words, take responsibility for them and clean them out, for it was you who put them there to begin with!

Too many people spend time whining about how they have been betrayed and hurt by close friends, their children and their spouses. It hurts. We all hurt from one time or another. But some almost take delight in wallowing in their sorrows and licking their wounds. Every single one of us has tough emotional blemishes in our lives, but whining will not get you out of harm's way. Your pursuit of the Path will necessarily force emotional blockages to the surface, and you in turn must toss them out and forget about them. You might even consider writing down these emotional pains on a piece of paper then burning it.

Both physical and emotional purification of the physical and astral vehicles will clear the way for your etheric faculties to come into play and thus ready you for the journey ahead. When the Spiritual Hierarchy signals the need to take a certain action, those with clear faculties, no matter where they are found in the world, will receive the call to action and will know what to do. This kind of communication cannot be

147

replaced by electronic communication or government agencies.

9. Balance the Masculine and Feminine Energies

As a lightbearer you should seek to balance the masculine and feminine energies within you. You are neither man nor woman but a soul expressing both masculine and feminine energies through a given body vehicle.

Unfortunately, the New Age Movement has misinterpreted the good news of the incoming feminine energies by equating them with the female gender. Some have even used this news to strike back at the male gender for all the past wrongs they have suffered as victims. Or some women have taken on an air of superiority as they combat male oppression or attempt to re-program their male friends.

The reprogramming needs to be done in your own thinking, for in reality, these energies, both masculine and feminine, have nothing to do with gender. They are soul qualities which everything expresses, not only humans but animals and plants.

To be an effective lightbearer, you must forget gender and all the "politics" that surround it. Let us avoid a backlash in the other extreme where the female gender dominates the male. Balance between these two categories of energies is the only way the Golden Age can achieve peace and tranquility.

10. Be Aware of the Release of Your Kundalini Energies

Taking the above preparatory steps will necessarily mean that your physical and emotional bodies will have to adjust to higher and higher vibrations as the pralaya advances. Reading and studying the Ancient Wisdom, meditating in concert with your Higher Self, and communicating with your Master will release the latent kundalini energies stored at the base of your spine. Your proper spiritual development provokes the release, not the other way round, i.e. artificial release of the kundalini will not make you more spiritual.

There are many views about this controversial subject from the outright crazy to the more prudent traditional yogic viewpoint. Some attribute every ailment they experience to the rising of their kundalini, while the more prudent and aware can physically sense the rising and receding of these energies over time. Each time it rises, it reaches for a higher chakra, then recedes for a period of rest and adjustment. The release of your kundalini energies is like a thermometer of your spiritual development.

Everyone experiences this release in a different way but it is unlikely that the release of kundalini energies up the spine will take place in one single coup. If this happens, the body vehicle would not be able to sustain it - it could be devastating. It is also unlikely that kundalini yoga manipulation would release these energies without the requisite spiritual development.

The kundalini release is more likely to come and go over a period of a couple years, and in the case of the lightbearer, your Master will supervise the release in tandem with the emergence of your Higher Self into your personality.

11. Progressively Move into More Advanced Meditation Techniques

The Sanctus Germanus Foundation will make available to lightbearers advanced meditation techniques at the right time. These advanced techniques are designed to help individuals maintain control over the mind during the stress and turmoil of the present pralaya. They will also help the individual stay in close mind contact with their Masters. Please check the Sanctus Germanus Foundation's website, www.sanctusgermanus.net for further details in the future.

The Inner Structure that Brings Us All Together

Whether consciously or unconsciously, you are *"held together by an inner structure of thought* and by a telepathic medium of interrelation. The Great Ones, Whom we all seek to serve, are thus linked, and can - at the slightest need and with the least expenditure of force - get en rapport with each other. They are all tuned to a particular vibration."[39]

These words give us comfort, for what we must face in the near future will not be a picnic. Lightbearers represent a wide diversity of soul experiences that add to the richness and depth of knowledge in the whole group. They come from

---

[39] Bailey, Alice B., *Telepathy and the Etheric Vehicle*, Lucis Trust, New York, p. 1

different countries, environments, heredities and traditions. Yet it is comforting to know that such a diverse group meets on common ground in the etheric where there is a meeting of minds and plans. How we bring this natural cooperation into play on the earth plane is the challenge that lies before us.

"In Him we live and move and have our being," in fact means *Omnipresence*. Omnipresence is a generic term covering the ocean of energies which are all interrelated and which constitute that one synthetic energy body of our planet. The etheric body of every form in nature is an integral part of the Creator's energies known as the form-making substance. The etheric or energy body, therefore, of every human being is an integral part of the etheric body of the planet itself and consequently of the solar system. Through this medium, every human being is basically related to every other expression of the Divine Life. [40]

You, who have consciously chosen to work with the Divine Plan during the earth changes, will have passed through emotional trials that will have strengthened your spiritual development and thus heightened your vibrations in tandem with the ever-higher vibrations on the earth plane. The synchronization with these higher vibrations will put you out of harm's way because the major battles of the Armageddon involve the higher vibrations agitating the lower. War and physical conflict involve the lowest vibrations that mankind can produce. The higher your vibrations, the farther you will be from harm's way.

---

[40] Ibid., p. 2

Spiritual development within the context of such changes will by necessity open your innate faculties to see etherically, communicate telepathically, and finally precipitate material needs. You can achieve the activation of these faculties through meditation, study, and unselfish service to humanity prior to 2012 through multiple religious or spiritual modalities available on the earth. In the next chapters, we will discuss how the revival of these faculties will play into your work in the Period of Reconstruction.

CHAPTER 6

Period of Reconstruction I

Creating Order out of Chaos

The meltdown or displacement of the ice caps and permafrost regions will continue at an accelerated pace post-2012. In the ashes of world war and economic depression, great floods will dominate life on earth hereon and force population displacements never seen in our history. Millions will choose to remain in harm's way and perish while others will flee to higher ground. Life on earth will be trying and chaotic, to say the least, and conditions will not favour the weak-hearted.

The World Situation in 2013

By 2013, the world will find itself in the throes of World War III. Any hope that the remnants of the Dark Forces have of reviving the economy will be dashed, so as they exit, the Dark Forces will release pandemics as a last ditch "scorched-earth" policy to ravage the planet - "If we cannot prevail, then we shall take all down with us" taking with them untold millions.

Those who have adjusted to the higher vibrations on earth will not be touched.

To challenge the earth's population further, earth changes will accelerate further, for the melting of the polar ice caps and vast permafrost regions will continue at an even more alarming rate. Sea levels will continue to rise and volatile storms will batter all continents with prolonged Noah-era-like rains that carry flooding inland and result in massive flooding of all lowland areas.

Major coastal and lowland cities (such as Hong Kong-Macau, Shanghai, Bangkok, Kolkata (Calcutta), Mumbai, Dubai, Cairo, Istanbul, Beirut, New York, London, Amsterdam, Brussels, Marseilles and others) will succumb to unprecedented flooding and human loss. Inland cities near major rivers or water bodies such as Chicago, Detroit, Toronto, Montreal, Frankfurt, and Paris will suffer the same fate.

By this time the deadly combination of war, pandemic diseases, poverty, and accelerated natural catastrophes will have already reduced the earth's population significantly. The confluence of these crises will have caused unprecedented worldwide suffering and casualties.

Upheaval and Regrouping

The general upheaval of the earth's population will bring into play the Laws of Attraction and Repulsion. Unlike other planets, earth has heretofore entertained a heterogeneous population comprised of lower evolutionary laggards from other planets and galaxies, rootless souls in the universe with no other place to go, remnants of past root-races, and human beings of very diverse sorts in various stages of spiritual development. This diversity has resulted in continuous conflicts that no other planet in the solar system experiences. The filtering out of the earth's population during this period due to incoming higher vibrations will activate these two cosmic laws and survivors will regroup accordingly.

Those who in self-preservation flee instinctively to higher ground will join those with whom they are compatible in accordance with these cosmic laws. Lightbearers driven by purpose and mission will eventually find their way to the more protected Spiritual Regions where those like-minded have gathered. There, they will meet others who through vision and foresight populated those areas in previous years.

Curiously, all survivors, although weary, are filled with hope and a new way of perceiving life. The thick muck of the astral plane will have thinned out considerably and more light will filter into the earth plane. The Dark Forces will have thinned out, and the critical mass of Light Forces will begin to outweigh them. Fresh inward flows of the Sun's life-giving energies, prana, will begin to resuscitate the earth plane and its etheric double, enabling people to breathe freely once again. Things will look and feel lighter and brighter despite the flooding. Finer etheric energies will permeate man's body and the soul will reach down to stimulate contact with his etheric body rather than the physical. As mankind further advances into the New Golden Age, this process will intensify.

By this time, the distinction between good and evil is clearly contrasted, and the good and innocent souls on earth begin to take charge. Astral plane influences linger, but its "colouring" of thought-forms is of a higher astral nature. Personal and selfish desires and emotions gradually give way to a need to serve others, this tendency evolving later into divine service. Much of the gratuitous "feel good" emotional sentimentality, the large swings between hatred and love and the perverse dark thoughts of violence gradually fade out. Literature, the arts and music blossom onto higher levels despite the world's turmoil and serve to elevate thinking in crisis rather than debase it. Society in general begins to seek the highest and the best instead of delving into the depths of depravity.

High Ground and the Spiritual Regions

The post-2012 period will change the geographical configuration of the earth's surface. As the floods gradually encroach, masses will ignore the initial signs and thus perish. Whilst many will listen to their intuitions well beforehand, it is unknown at this time how many will choose to survive.

The general population will naturally seek refuge on higher ground that is closest to the flooded areas. Lightbearers and their disciples, on the other hand, will follow their intuitions and repair to designated Spiritual Regions, well before the actual floods hit their areas. The Spiritual Regions are all quite far from the coastal areas and located on high plateaux on every continent. Picking up and moving to these will require a high degree of commitment and faith.

Adepts of secret mystical societies linked to the regional branches of the Spiritual Hierarchy have already begun moving into these Spiritual Regions under cover of other identities in preparation for the events ahead. These societies have maintained the pure mystical teachings of the Spiritual Hierarchy throughout the centuries from which the various exoteric religions known today have sprouted.

Higher Elevation Zones

Millions of lowland survivors fleeing to higher ground will begin the onerous task of rebuilding and survival with little or no help from their governments. A general state of anarchy will exist until groups form and develop rules of survival. Small colonies, scattered among the foothills of today's present mountain ranges, will organise themselves in line with the Law of Attraction.

The higher elevation safe zones will provide temporary sanctuary, however they will be subject to continuing and more profound earth changes as projected in Stage 3 (See Chapter 3). The only areas that will survive further change will be the twelve Spiritual Regions designated by the Spiritual Hierarchy. These regions will grow over time into large, advanced, spiritually-anchored civilisations that will draw their populations from the surrounding areas.

Years 2013 to 2020 will prove the most difficult and chaotic period of our transition scenario. Surviving populations will endure a state of constant flux as the sea, rivers, lakes, and other water bodies take over lowland areas. Heavy, steady rains will flood interiors. Only skeletons of governments will remain, and these will be rendered useless. Local jurisdictional authorities will be forced to rely on their own means to maintain law and order and generate mutual aid groups among the displaced. Where this is not possible, anarchy will exist, counting on the basic good instincts of mankind to maintain order in a chaotic situation.

Many high elevation urban areas will be left intact, and large numbers of displaced persons will head toward these areas. Local governments in these high elevation areas will have to cope with thousands upon thousands of refugees and provide them with basic needs. The magnitude of resettlement will be so great that only well-organized mutual aid groups and local government will be able to implement solutions, frequently depending upon the generosity and initiative of local residents.

With the breakdown of laws, contracts, ownership rights, and general societal order, survivors will have little to depend on, bar seeking out those of similar vibration. At this point, natural cosmic laws, and not the law of the jungle, will automatically take over. Ad hoc groups will form in accordance with the Law of Attraction. Freedom to live and associate with whomever and wherever one pleases will prevail. In this way, small groups will form to protect one another and survive in the elevated safe zones.

As higher elevation zones struggle to re-establish order and settle the displaced, lightbearers will continue to make their way to the twelve Spiritual Regions, where their fellows and members of the Spiritual Hierarchy will have gathered to begin the reconstruction process based on cosmic laws. Order will emerge from chaos as fast as the Spiritual Regions can consolidate and establish themselves, for these Spiritual Regions will lead the way to reshape society for the New Golden Age.

Twelve Spiritual Regions: Twelve Experiments

In previous sub-rounds, there have existed great spiritual civilisations in which there occurred active interplay between the spiritual dimensions and the earth plane. These regions, such as China and Mesopotamia, flourished with little contact one with another. Previous Golden Age civilisations such as the one headed by an earlier incarnation of the Master Sanctus Germanus in what is today known as the Sahara desert, flourished under cosmic law.[41] Their inhabitants lived under a regime of peace and tranquility, and many Masters were borne out of these civilisations.

In a return to this ancient tradition, the Spiritual Hierarchy has designated twelve Spiritual Regions to serve as seed territories out of which the Golden Age civilisation will bloom on each continent. These twelve Spiritual Regions will constitute pockets of order amidst chaos and be governed according to cosmic law. The promised Golden Age is not expected to be global, but will take place in these centres. This is because the rest of the world will be in the throes of geological adjustments.

------

[41] See Godfre Ray King, *Unveiled Mysteries*, St. Germain Press: Schaumburg, Illinois, pp. 33-71.

Together, these Regions will constitute a nexus of energy portals from which the Hierarchy will communicate its plan for the reorganization of human society and laying of the groundwork for the long-awaited manifestation of the World Teacher, whose appearance in whatever form deemed feasible at the time, is expected around 2020. Adepts of the regional branches of the Brotherhood of Light will emerge from the inner planes to help lightbearers consolidate in these Regions.

In the Spiritual Regions, lightbearers along with adepts of the Spiritual Hierarchy will build a transitional society that will experiment with the best of our current civilisation and new ideas flowing in from the Spiritual Hierarchy in order to create a working model for the New Golden Age. These centres of spiritual erudition and power will be modeled upon Shamballa, the headquarters of the Spiritual Hierarchy. Each region will become a beacon of light for its continent, and each will represent a new form of aspiration, based on spiritual development.

People living in the surrounding areas will aspire to go to the Spiritual Regions to live under an enlightened regime. No longer will money and material wealth be defined as primary aspirations of mankind. All will be welcome, provided they demonstrate the required level of spiritual development. If they do not, the higher vibrations of these areas will be too much to bear and will naturally repel them. The higher vibrations will protect these Spiritual Regions from unwanted incursions, as a state of duality will continue to exist on earth.

From each Spiritual Region will come the basis for law and order for a particular area, taking into account racial and cultural characteristics. As the Spiritual Regions gain in stature, they will constitute both the administrative and representative spiritual hierarchy for each area. Colonies in the higher elevation zones surrounding these Spiritual Regions will be given the choice to emulate or integrate into this hierarchical reorganization.

To reiterate, the twelve *Spiritual Regions* of the world have been revealed as follows:

North America:
(1) Banff-Lake Louise area near Calgary, Canada to the Grand Tetons area of Wyoming, USA
(2) Colorado Plateau area

South America:
(3)The Cordoba Province in Argentina and
(4) The Goias Province in Brazil

East Asia:
(5) Qinghai-Tibet Plateau and
(6) Gobi Desert Plateau

South Asia:
(7) Darjeeling area including Sikkim in the Himalayas Foothills

Australia:
(8) The Australian Outback region

Middle East:
(9) Iran plateau near Yazd, Iran

Africa:
(10) the Central Highlands Lake Kivu area and
(11) the Ahaggar Plateau near Tamanrasset, Algeria

Europe:
(12) Transylvanian Plateau in the Carpathian Mountains

Weather patterns will change rapidly and radically in the decades to come and will make such forbidden areas as the Australian Outback, Saharan Plateau, and the Gobi plateau much more habitable. A very mild, humid climate is expected to dominate, and regular rainfall will resume in arid regions that were once fertile. Those who have lived in desert areas have already noted that when any rain falls, the desert immediately springs to life.

The Thirteenth Spiritual Region: Capital of the New Golden Age

The thirteenth Spiritual Region will be designated the Capital of the New Golden Age around the year 2040. Two locations may be considered: Victoria Island in the Northern reaches of Canada, or Greenland. What is revealed after the glaciers have melted and how these two locations are affected by the world war will determine whether either of them meets the karmic requirements of the Spiritual Hierarchy for such a sacred location.

Reconstruction in the Spiritual Regions Defined

Deep contemplation and meditation by the adepts of the Spiritual Hierarchy who have followed the flight to the Spiritual Regions will bring forth the Period of Reconstruction. The catastrophic earth changes of the pralaya will have destroyed the obvious symbols and institutions that did not serve mankind, but mankind is not expected to rebuild the same civilisation as implied in the word "reconstruction." Reconstruction means the rebuilding of only that which will serve us based on solid experience of the past millennia. It will involve the culling out of the bad and rebuilding of the good—a second chance granted to right that which went wrong.

Pralaya means "a period of obscuration, destruction and rest." Rest is a critical characteristic of a pralaya, but does not imply that mankind will loll around and do nothing. The cosmic laws that govern a pralaya period are designed to balance those active periods of creation. Rest is a time to take stock of what has been accomplished, evaluate what went right and what went wrong and to learn what to keep and what to reject. It is very much like the evaluation phase of a project cycle. Once a project has terminated, evaluators seek to find out if it had reached its goals and if not, to learn why it did not. Herein lies the real lessons that the soul must contemplate and reflect upon. So rather than being tossed about in the stormy seas of progress, change, trial and error, the soul rests in the calm waters of contemplation and evaluation.

Those incarnating during the pralaya will not be as blind as those previous. Their ability to call up past lives and read the akashic records on the mental plane will be enhanced so that a review of how their past lives through other active creative periods might contribute to the New Golden Age.

The Period of Reconstruction reaches for great profundity. Like a gift from heaven, therein is given the opportunity to RE-construct that which should have been on a surer footing. This is the essence of the meaning of Reconstruction.

Cosmic Laws Governing Spiritual Regions

The Master Sanctus Germanus thought and meditated deeply on this pralaya centuries before the actual catastrophic events began. Other Masters, their initiates, and lightbearers pored over plans and details in preparation, too. Nothing was left to random circumstance, except for the free will exercised by mankind. Order WILL emerge out of chaos in the Spiritual Regions, if lightbearers heed the directives to go to these regions well in advance of the mass population displacements and work with the adepts of the Hierarchy to create the structure that will bring order to a society in flux. All cosmic laws already known to mankind will remain in effect, as they are eternal as the universe. Understanding them is another question. Further to these laws, we wish to introduce a new set of cosmic laws pertaining to periods of destruction and rest such as this pralaya.

The Transitional Society

The inhabitants of the Spiritual Regions will organize a transitional society that will experiment with organisations and institutions based on cosmic law. It is called "transitional" because of its experimental nature. The model that emerges from this experiment will be used to create the much-promised New Golden Age.

The ultimate purpose of a society is to allow souls to express themselves freely through their respective physical body vehicles. Through education, meditation, and service within a structure of cosmic laws, a society can in itself achieve this "Soul Liberation".

Cosmic laws will provide a legal structure adapted to prevailing conditions. They will form an umbrella of principles, much like a constitution, but more in line with true universal principles. From these broad principles, human regulations can be fitted to handle local requirements.

Cosmic law is not written on paper. It is ingrained in the very fabric of each soul. Everything moves and exists within a lawful structure of rules and cycles. As such, when the soul is liberated in each individual, the basic pattern of law and self-enforcement becomes manifest. Proper application and implementation of cosmic law requires no police or military, no arms to coerce or force compliance, and no arbitrary decisions based on individual notions of law enforcement. Rather it is law and enforcement within, combined as one, a joy in the heart that realizes its obligations within the framework of creation and gives one that sense of peace and security so sought after in today's world.

As souls are liberated, the knowledge of cosmic law will come into being. The volumes of laws that fill law libraries covering every criminal act will lose their basis since those acts, which fundamentally mirror mankind's divergence from cosmic law, will no longer prevail. Teachings from the Spiritual Hierarchy will correct mistaken notions of cosmic laws brought over from today's civilisation and together the learning process on all levels of society will ensue with urgency.

Cosmic laws not yet articulated will then be introduced to the transitional society and tried. How the transitional society will adapt to these laws is unknown at this time. Experimentation of this nature will be fundamental to the building of a New Golden Age.

The set of cosmic laws below characterize the mindset that humanity must adopt during a period of pralaya and how reconstruction should be viewed. Whilst they may appear very similar to one another, there are subtle differences.

1. The Law of Attraction

Like binds to like. The earth will no longer be the free dumping ground of disparate levels of evolutions. It will no longer be possible for an individual who is disconnected from his soul to incarnate on earth as so many have done in the Dark Forces-dominated era. Earth's higher vibrations will automatically prevent this. In the beginning, this phenomenon may manifest in the number of stillbirths or babies who do not survive while parents are adjusting to higher vibrations. This should not cause alarm to survivors, as it must be seen as the best way to stop intrusive attempts into the new physical plane. After a period of time, incarnations will flow into higher vibratory vehicles as per plan.

The implication of this law in creating harmonious vehicles is without question one of the most important, for it acts as a sort of cosmic immigration policy that will continue to filter out lower evolutions. There are other planets in the infinite number of solar systems upon which it would be more suitable for them to find form.

Homogeneity in vibration is thus the result of the more stringent application of the Law of Attraction, although its influence will not cause all mankind to look alike. In fact the varieties and colours of the various vehicles will increase and astound present humanity —blue, green, red — yet the vibratory compatibility will harmonize all relations so that colour is not used as a criterion for discrimination but rather as a contribution of quality to the society - in essence a more complete expression of the mass soul. The difference in colour will be primarily seen on the physical level, however on the etheric level colour will fade into the harmony of finer matter.

Individuals operating on similar and higher vibratory levels can accomplish so much more than heterogeneous groups. Imagine groups inherently agreeing to certain objectives within the Divine Plan and working harmoniously in concert with one another! Such is rare, if not unthinkable today. The like-minded will gather and work together, and communities will form likewise according to the mutual attractiveness of their members. No one will be forced or coerced to join or work with people of dissimilar tendencies and characteristics, the freedom to choose or return to one's ashram being preserved and guaranteed in this Law.

2. Law of Repulsion (the converse)

This law also applies and thus forms the borders or limits of a group activity. Therefore, the group has certain geographical and policy limitations to assure non-dominance over others or the use of force to control and artificially hold people together. The Law of Repulsion thus sets the limits of group action and assures diversity among groups. However, even in this diversity, there will be threads of common interest among groups that will bond these groups within the limitations imposed by this Law.

3. Law of Cosmic Spontaneity

What is cosmic spontaneity but the bursting forth of soul knowledge rather than deliberate and measured action? Much of this spontaneity is seen in children today, and it taps into Divine Intelligence in the most direct and positive way.

This law is connected to telepathic communication, for it is spontaneity that assures the purest form of thought transference. A thought-form dropped into your mind becomes instantly recognizable and digested. It is instant comprehension in its purest form. Human posturing and thinking over thought-forms invariably twists the original meanings and causes distortions that later experience must remove. Cosmic spontaneity has much to do with the saying "quicker than a ray of light."

Such spontaneity works best when the astral body is under control and the physical vehicle (both dense physical and etheric) is in direct contact with the mental and causal bodies.

4. The Law of Perpetual Action

Everything is in motion. This law recognizes that all of creation is perpetually changing, and that there is no place for laziness or for subjecting others to do the grunt work. So those who recognize this law will let go of tradition and the old ways and open themselves to the ever-evolving ideas that flow from the hierarchy.

There is a mindset among certain individuals that growth stops at a certain age. They adopt styles and ways of thinking that are comfortable or traditional. Many stop growing intellectually and mentally. But with an understanding of perpetual dynamism so engrained in the new society, hanging on to tradition will give way to reception of the ever-flowing supply of divine ideas in the new order.

5. The Law of Perpetual Fluidity and Malleability

The contrary concept to this law is a materialistic mindset that wishes to anchor all ideas in some solid or stable form. Fluidity and malleability bring a higher and subtler taste for the spiritual, *ever-seeking*, ever-adaptable, ever able to drop that which no longer serves, letting go that which encumbers. It is openness of mind at its best.

6. The Law of Abandonment

Ideas and thought-forms abound in the universe, all for man's use. They circulate freely as resources to be used toward Soul Liberation or to be abandoned or let go for others to use. Clinging to ideas as forever right, however much they were in their time, retards growth and progress. Being able to let go when the right time comes is a peek into what true freedom is all about. When you let go, you do so because your soul prompts you to something better. Why not move on to better? Why cling to what is comfortable and safe when a new idea could be even more comfortable and safer? It is the upheaval when adopting the new that people try to avoid but to welcome change and upheaval as part of the ever-continuing life spectrum is to know that abandoning something that has passed its usefulness is a cosmic law of progress.

7. Law of Upheaval

We mentioned that the transition from the old to the new always involves upheaval in one's life. The more one is used to change and adheres to the need for change and allows new ideas to permeate one's life, tossing away what is no longer useful, the more one becomes accustomed to upheaval during transition. This is part of the cyclic nature of the universe. This empowering law is to be respected and endured, not avoided or outgrown.

8. The Law of Constant Renewal

Cycles come and go but one thing is certain, as we throw off that which is not useful, renewal takes hold, re-establishing tranquility and pouring new energies in to renew one's life. This is part of the eternal cycle that many reactionary minds today use to prevent renewal. Yet renewal is the completion of the cycle and must come into play before anything can continue. Trying to stop the end of the cycle stymies progress.

The Law of Constant Renewal is related to the Law of Abundance and constant supply; however, this supply comes in cycles as with all things and when exhausted, is renewed.

You can't have it all at once, but you will have it all when the right time and place requires it and that is usually at the beginning of a cycle. The flow of abundance is not heaped on one willy nilly or all at once but in carefully measured cyclical steps.

9. Law of Synchronicity

As the earth shifts position so will mankind's perception of the zodiac, which has played a major role through astrology in understanding the timing of events. Time, thus, will continue on the earth plane and into the New Golden Age. But time will be governed by certain goals set in the Divine Plan, which in turn is synchronized with the perception of the new zodiac.

The melting of the ice caps is an indication of the shift in the north-south axis of the earth, and this gradual shift will require adjustments in man's perception of the planetary interplay and its influence on earth activities.

The Divine Plan for the Spiritual Regions is synchronized with planetary interplay and thus a modified astrology will reflect this new synchronization of time. There are blocks of cycles when certain Plan goals must be achieved, and the events and activities will intermesh accordingly in a synchronized fashion. Time must be reckoned in terms of these cycles and not according to mankind's clock.

Mankind's role is to recognize this interplay and choose his action among many in accordance with these blocks of synchronicity. Thus, a more passive approach to life characterizes a pralaya and allows for the timing of events to unfold in terms of the Divine Plan. Allowing the Plan to unfold as scheduled is to allow the Law of Synchronicity to unfold. A new breed of astrologers is needed to unlock this law and interpret it for the people.

The active and wilful activity conforming to some arbitrarily determined time agenda that so characterized the present era, for example conquests and aggressive warmongering, will not take place during a pralaya. Mankind must learn to detach from wilful activity -to step back and allow the Law of Synchronicity to take hold and manifest.

10. The Law of Divine Momentum

Divine momentum is the recognition that with the Plan comes the force or will of implementation. Every element or provision of the Divine Plan possesses the inherent power to manifest on the earth plane. As the planetary interplay begins to unlock certain blocks or cycles of unfoldment, a momentum of implementation takes over, built within the Plan. This sets into action certain activities that the Spiritual Hierarchy will externalize on earth, which in turn will create right activity for its earthly counterparts. Together the Plan is realized, but it is up to mankind to join and cede to the momentum of implementation.

Individuals are given the freedom to choose activities that either promote or thwart such a momentum. To be in concert with the implementation momentum is to open up infinite opportunities for service, whereas to thwart it pits the individual soul against it. Recognizing that there is a momentum and joining in puts man in harmony with the Plan for the forces that would thwart the Plan will eventually be dissipated. Contrary action will be viewed as a violation of cosmic Law.

Reconstruction in the Spiritual Regions will require such momentum, otherwise evolution will stall. So in a sense, passive adherence to the force as built into the Plan during a pralaya will result in reconstructive activity that is not "new" activity but more a righting or correction of what should have transpired. To be in the spirit of the Plan requires mankind to interfere less with the Plan and cede to its momentum. As reconstruction efforts mirror those foreseen in the Divine Plan, they will achieve the Divine momentum needed to manifest themselves within the cycle of time allotted as defined by the timing of planetary interplay.

This momentum will be mirrored in the new astrology to be developed in the Spiritual Regions. It is not the change in the universe that man observes but the change in his position and perception. Divine momentum will thus be understood and mapped out in the new astrology.

11. The Law of Passive Adherence

This law underlies all activity during periods of pralaya. The present era views passivity as a negative

173

characteristic. The result of aggressive activity has built much in the way of concrete structure, research, and innovative ideas. However, much that has been created must be evaluated in terms of the Divine Plan. Active creativity gives way to passive wisdom in the New Golden Age. Wisdom is that which evaluates creativity in terms of its usefulness and evolutionary benefits to mankind.

Passive adherence to the Plan gives recognition to a right structure into which man's creativity can be funnelled for the benefit of the whole. The wisdom that streams forth from the Plan must be recognized and used to evaluate that which was created in the present era, superseding rugged individualism. Absorbing and understanding the Plan anchors its principles and laws to the point that the bad will naturally spin out and the good be retained around them.

For a person to adhere to this cosmic law, the mental body must be developed. A cultivated intellect is required to understand the deep sense of wisdom. Thus, passive adherence implies active mental activity versus physical action. And these mental activities focus on evaluation of the past, adoption of what is useful and beneficial to that which was created in the present era, and the invocation of wisdom needed to implement that which has been culled from the past.

Passive adherence to the Divine Plan thus enables evaluation and brings to the surface that which conforms to the Plan's principles of wisdom. In this process there is still activity, but it is passive because it is defined and restrained by wisdom.

12. The Law of Reverse Motion

In line with what we have said about the period of pralaya, much of what is progress is a recapitulation and evaluation of what was created during the preceding active period i.e. culling out the bad and retaining the good. By reversing general motion, we are actually moving forward with the good and positive. The elimination of that which is not useful for mankind makes space to emphasize and expand the positive. In linear thinking, reverse motion would imply retrogression, and in a sense this is correct but in the multi-dimensional thinking, reverse means making room for the good to expand. Think upon this.

13. Law of Containment

The filtering out of that which is not useful to mankind must be done with the utmost wisdom. In some instances, the choice is obvious, that certain institutions or human laws are in blatant violation to their cosmic counterpart. But in most instances the choice involves thought-forms that have not fully germinated or were twisted in meaning upon their descent into matter. Thus, they never realized their full potential.

Containment in this instance means preservation of that which is good within thought-forms that have not realized their full potential, but if set loose within the present context, would have been detrimental to mankind. One instance of this is the unleashing of atomic energy, the full use of which has been contained for fear of misuse. Mankind has taken some thought-forms to their logical extremes resulting in great suffering. Many wars are justified by taking to extremes high principles.

The culling out of the old and bad must take place within certain limitations of wisdom; otherwise we will have so-called revolutionary or fanatical witch-hunts and scapegoats against that which is old. Certain traditions of the past are fully realized thought-forms that are meant to endure no matter what, while others are of suspect origin and do not serve mankind. There is a huge grey area of thought-forms primarily in the realm of high technology. They seemingly have some benefit that can be realized but can also be used to the detriment of mankind. The Law of Containment limits excessive, fanatical directions that certain thought-forms can take.

14. Law of Abatement

Abatement is the ending, reduction or lessening of something. The excesses of mankind in certain directions can in part be attributed to the battle of the Dark Forces to maintain their position on earth at all cost. Many thought-forms started out based on high ideals only to be extended to the point of excess. Technology enabled mankind to extend himself beyond the limitations of his body vehicle, but all have been abused to the ends of the Dark Forces. Yet the technology remains at its core beneficial to mankind. Eliminating the innovative thought-form is not the solution. Using wisdom to abate the excess and preserve the essence of the thought-form is what this law of pralaya aims at. It is very much part of the genre of laws that restrain and contain the excesses of the present era and is linked to the Law of

Containment. Concrete thinking in matter has been pushed to its limit in the post World War II period, and the gentle rain of wisdom will rein in that which is useful and eliminate some excesses.

15. Law of Consolidation

The creative activities of the Fourth Sub-Round have lasted for millennia and the present Fifth Root-Race generated so much activity that historical and patent archives are overflowing. The Dark Forces exerted much energy to suppress many of these revolutionary thought-forms.

These thought-forms must be revisited, digested and not forgotten in their entirety—the good and beneficial must be extracted, evaluated, firmly anchored, and tried. Much of the Twentieth-Century has been fleeting - an endless search for something new, but that which has been given has not yet been fully digested, and mankind has not fully tested a multitude of thought-forms before moving on to the next.

The period of pralaya that we have started is not one of random destruction but more one of filtration--casting out the unwanted and bad and consolidating the good and pure. It is also active rest to digest thought-forms for the New Golden Age.

CHAPTER 7

Period of Reconstruction II

Towards An Etheric Existence

As lightbearers move to the Spiritual Regions, they will organize and reconstruct society along the lines of a new cosmic order. These Regions will stand as beacons of hope and aspiration for human society. Those who started on the probationary path in previous lifetimes will feel drawn to them, while those who have no interest in spiritual matters despite the catastrophes will rebuild their lives as best they can, in peripheral elevated zones.

The Spiritual Regions are areas of high vibration that the Spiritual Hierarchy has designated for the survival of human civilisation during the pralaya. They are vast enough to absorb the majority of survivors and by their light will attract a constant inflow from the general population in accordance with the cosmic Law of Attraction. Spiritual Regions are not exclusive areas, but stops on the evolutionary path. On each continent, they will serve as new aspirations for survivors, a place where they will go to live in peace, harmony, brotherhood, and abundance.

The requirements for all who enter the Spiritual Regions are the same as for the Path of Initiation: the probationary path, the way of the disciple and the four grades of initiation. The majority of survivors will have moved to higher elevations out of instinct for self-preservation. A minority will already be on the probationary path, i.e. "on the side of the forces of evolution, and working at the building of his own character . . ." [42]and will be more apt to seek refuge in the Spiritual Regions.

> He takes himself in hand, cultivates the qualities that are lacking in his disposition, and seeks with diligence to bring his personality under control. He is building the causal body with deliberate intent, filling any gaps that may exist, and seeking to make it a fit receptacle for the Christ principle. [43]

Characteristics of the Spiritual Regions

The Spiritual Regions are in essence dimensional portals to the etheric plane, where the Spiritual Hierarchy will communicate with its earthly counterparts of lightbearers, disciples, and probationers. In these regions, residents will straddle earth's dense physical and etheric planes and will build a transitional society marked by inter-dimensional communication.

In order for residents to take full advantage of these regions, they will need to regain many faculties

---

[42] Bailey, Alice A., *Initiation Human and Solar*, p. 65
[43] Ibid.

associated with the etheric body, such as telepathy, clairvoyance, and etheric vision. And as the years go by, residents in these regions will function more and more on the etheric plane using their etheric bodies as their physical vehicle of expression.

Lightbearers who have cleared their astral bodies during the initial turmoil of the pralaya will be the first to function with the etheric as their form vehicle. This is because the etheric body will have clearer access to the mental body through a cleansed astral and vice versa, and mankind will rely more on its thinking abilities than emotions. The astral body will still play a role in shaping mankind's thinking in the higher forms of astral colouring, for example higher aspirations and expression of arts and music and the desire for service rather than self gratification. So one could say that the main characteristic of transitional society in the Spiritual Regions will be the gradual change of form expression from the dense physical to the etheric. Depending on the spiritual acuity of each Spiritual Region, this phase could take decades or centuries.

The shape of the transitional society, its structures and *modus operandi*, are to be determined entirely by its inhabitants working in concert with their counterparts in the Spiritual Hierarchy. Free will will predominate, as mankind is given an incredible opportunity to reshape its entire existence based on past experience and the introduction of new innovative thought-forms. This is the grand perspective to which only survivors of the present society can contribute; hence the critical role of the lightbearers.

The transitional society is a grand experiment and its outcome is not guaranteed. The Middle East, once a major spiritual dimensional portal that spawned great civilisations, has degenerated into a region of major conflict in today's world. So if mankind is not vigilant, it may still alter the thought-forms generated by the Planetary Logos, the Masters of Wisdom and their initiates, even without the presence of the Dark Forces, and lead the Spiritual Regions down a dark path. It has happened many times before.

This time, however, is slightly different given so many incarnated initiates expected to keep in close communication with the Spiritual Hierarchy.

Backdrop of Geological Changes

The creation of the transitional society will take place over many decades, even as geological changes slowly convulse and cleanse other parts of the earth. As mankind gradually enters the New Golden Age, both the earth's astral plane and man's astral body will gradually be eliminated, and earth life will move onto the etheric plane. In the meantime, the Spiritual Regions will serve as prototypes for what earth is to become over the coming centuries, so the kind of society mankind creates in these regions will affect the shape and fabric of the New Golden Age.

Role of Gold in the Spiritual Regions

Gold is expected to play a major role in the Spiritual Regions, not only as a means of exchange but also for its esoteric value in purifying, balancing and vitalizing energies. Here is a statement about gold that the Master Sanctus Germanus made many decades ago:

Gold was a common commodity . . . in all Golden Ages, because its natural emanation is a purifying, balancing, and vitalizing energy or force. It is placed within the earth by the 'Lords to Creation'-- those 'Great Beings Of Life and Love' who create and direct worlds, systems of worlds, and the expansion of the light in the beings upon them.

The outer or intellectual knowledge of humanity holds within it little - very little - understanding of the real purpose for which gold exists on this planet. It grows within the earth like a plant, and through it there is constantly pouring a purifying, vitalizing balance and current of energy into the very ground we walk upon, as well as into the growth of nature and the atmosphere we breathe.

Gold is placed upon this planet for a variety of uses, two of its most trivial and unimportant ones being that of using gold as a means of exchange and for ornamentation. The far greater activity and purpose of it, within and upon the earth, is the release of its own inherent quality and energy to purify, vitalize and balance the atomic structure of the world.

The scientific world today has no inkling as yet of this activity. However, it serves the same purpose to our earth that radiators do to our homes. Gold is one of the most important ways by which the energy from our sun is supplied to the interior of the earth, and the balance of activities maintained. As a conveyor of this energy, it acts as a transformer to pass the sun's force into the physical substance of our world, as well as to the life evolving upon it. The energy within gold is really the radiant, electronic force from the sun, acting in a lower octave. Gold is sometimes called a precipitated sun-ray.

As the energy within gold is of extremely high vibratory rate, it can only act upon the finer and more subtle expressions of life, through absorption. In all "Golden Ages," this metal comes into plentiful and common use by the mass of the people, and whenever

183

such a condition occurs, the spiritual development of that people reaches a very high state. In these ages, the gold is *never* hoarded but instead, is widely distributed into the use of the masses who, absorbing its purifying energy, are themselves raised into greater perfection. Such is the right use of gold, and when this Law is consciously understood and obeyed, the individual may draw any quantity he desires to himself by the use of that Law.

Because of the gold deposits in all mountain ranges, one finds health and vigour in life upon the mountains that he cannot find in any other place on the earth's surface. No one ever heard of detrimental effects coming to those who constantly handle pure gold. While in its pure state, it is soft and wears away easily, still the very quality is the fulfilling of this purpose of which I have just spoken.

The more advanced of these people produced much gold by *precipitation* direct from the Universal. The domes of many buildings were covered with sheets of pure gold and the interiors decorated with brilliant jewels in curious yet marvelous designs. These jewels were also precipitated--direct from the One Eternal Substance. "[44]

It is assumed that each Spiritual Region will be endowed with an abundance of gold, and has been designated for this reason.

Free Energy in the Spiritual Regions

In line with the esoteric importance of gold, the modes of exploiting an unlimited supply of free energy electro-magnetically from natural energy vibrations that surround us will be revealed and unleashed in these Regions. Tapping into this free source of energy

---

[44] King, Godfre Ray, op.cit., pp. 44-46

has been known for eons, but the Dark Forces have severely suppressed this knowledge in order to perpetuate a regime of fossil fuels linked to their money-making enterprises.

Proponents of free energy will bring their technology to the Spiritual Regions where it will be released for the benefit of the society. Again, the custodians of this technology are lightbearers.

The positive and moderating vibrations of gold's presence, coupled with an unlimited source of free energy in the Spiritual Regions, promise to lift a heavy burden off the backs of mankind and enable it to concentrate more on the spiritual path as opposed to struggling daily for survival.

Lightbearers in the Spiritual Regions

The Spiritual Hierarchy has always recognized that an individual's spiritual evolution can outpace the evolution of mankind. This is why the Planetary Logos set up the Path of Initiation millions of years ago. The ranks of the earth's Spiritual Hierarchy are now filled with ordinary human beings who chose this Path and passed through the rigors of countless incarnations to qualify.

As the Dark Forces are expelled from the earth, the doors to the Probationary Path will be swung wide open to give all survivors equal opportunity to begin the journey of ascension. Indeed, we estimate that most of the survivors will already have begun this journey in previous lifetimes and have been "fence sitters" during this incarnation.

Lightbearers of all grades and their disciples who make their way to the Spiritual Regions will encounter higher vibrations that will bring out many latent abilities and enhance their work as White Magicians. These etheric qualities will shape the transitional society they create.

Reduction of Astral Plane Influences

The higher vibrations of the dimensional portals will necessarily stimulate the etheric body and thus reopen faculties that mankind has long forgotten. In order that the etheric body play its true role as the controller of the dense physical body, the blockages posed by the astral body must be swept away. This is one of the main results of the present filtering process of what is called the Armageddon.

By the time reconstruction begins in the Spiritual Regions, the astral body and plane will have undergone a major cleansing of the malevolent influences connected to the Dark Forces. The heaviness of the atmosphere we feel today will be lightened as the grossest of astral matter is cleansed or eliminated. Mankind can now entertain more clearly and with less astral colouring the higher ideas or thought-forms being transmitted from the causal body to the mental and then to the etheric body. However, for many decades to come, the astral body, although diminished in its influence, will continue to colour thought-forms with astral colour and sentiments of a nostalgic nature, until mankind lets go of pre-pralaya era memories and chooses consciously to work with thoughts flowing from the mental plane. This is a process of education that will take place in the Spiritual Regions.

The purer thoughts of the mental plane are made up of a finer etheric matter that the astral can never mimic. The etheric body is quite receptive to them as they convey a satisfaction and wholeness that astral thought has never given mankind. There is a danger that once the astral plane has been cleansed of the negative, those good, romantic and sentimental thought-forms left over will lull mankind into a plateau of ease and obscure the higher thought-forms from the mental plane. It is in this way that the astral plane will remain both an unconscious and conscious reality in the minds of mankind for decades, perhaps centuries.

Its form will not resemble what we have today — a thick, mucky heavy layer - but more a benign thin layer above the etheric. Those in the Spiritual Regions will gradually gain an acute ability to distinguish between mental and astral thought-forms, and this ability will of course depend on mankind's receptivity to the Spiritual Hierarchy's new education. It is expected that there will not be any shortcuts to the cleansing of the astral plane and body, but that the process will continue for many more decades, perhaps centuries, until they no longer exist. The elimination of the astral plane will be a marked characteristic of the New Golden Age.

Growing Importance of the Etheric Body

Many early occultists treated the etheric body as "the etheric double" or that lighter, physical form that formed energy fields around the physical body and objects, which was responsible for drawing the sun's energy into the physical body. The Chinese call this *qi*, the Hindus *prana*, modern science *bioplasma*. Today, scientists recognize its existence as do those with etheric vision or clairvoyance. The etheric double was considered more an appendage of the physical rather than a body of its own intelligence like the astral or mental bodies. However, the teachings of the Master Djwal Khul through Alice A. Bailey reversed this perception and stated that *the etheric body is in reality the true form vehicle, and the physical body is merely its automaton.* In other words, the etheric body exerts control over and interpenetrates, underlies and occupies the entire physical organism. It also extends beyond the physical form and surrounds it like an aura.[45] Those with clairvoyant faculties can observe the etheric body as plainly as one sees the physical body. Others with developed clairsentient faculties can actually feel it with their hands.

As we embark on the creation of the transitional society, the etheric body will emerge as the primary form of expression and the faculties associated with this body will play a role in shaping an entirely different society based on the good of the past and the insight of the mankind's enhanced faculties.

Five Etheric Faculties in the Spiritual Regions

Advanced lightbearers who settle in the Spiritual Regions will have already developed to a high degree their etheric faculties as part of their reawakening. In the higher vibrational setting of the Spiritual Regions, they will find that these faculties will blossom. Others along the Path of Initiation who move to the Spiritual Regions will discover that their spiritual development advances at a much quicker pace.

---

[45] It is said that one's evolutionary level determines how far the etheric body extends out from the physical body.

The five etheric faculties — etheric vision, telepathic communication, continuity of consciousness, multi-dimensional thinking, and precipitation - are presently more widespread than one imagines. One need only consider the number of psychics, mediums, intuitives, sensitives, and those who respond to a keen "sixth sense". These are the lightbearers. One must also note that these faculties are very much developed in the incoming new race, the Sixth Root-Race.

Etheric Vision

Etheric vision is defined as the physical eye's ability to see life on the etheric plane. The dense material plane on which we base most of our perceptions through the five senses is nothing more than an illusion. Reality, or life's true material manifestion, exists on the etheric plane or the etheric double of earth. The Master Djwal Khul states the following:

> Etheric vision, or the power to see energy-substance, is true vision for the human being, just as the etheric is the true form. But until the race is further evolved, the eye is aware of and responds to the heavier vibration only. Gradually it will shake itself free from the lower and coarser reactions, and become an organ of true vision. [46]

Many people today possess the ability to see etherically. There are a growing number of psychics and mediums as well as those practicing various modalities of energy healing who can either sense, see or feel *prana* or energy fields that constitute the etheric

---

[46] Bailey, Alice A. *Treatise on Cosmic Fire*, New York: Lucis Publishing, p. 1096.

body. Some can see the complex energy matrices and the dynamic interaction of these energy matrices surrounding living objects such as trees and plants. Etheric vision is, thus, the highest form of physical eyesight, and it will constitute a major new dimension that people will explore in the transitional society.

As the astral plane gradually fades out, the etheric reality that has been shrouded by the physical plane illusion will come more to light, and through the sense of etheric vision, people of the New Golden Age will perceive things and objects as energy shapes rather than as the solid objects we see today. A house will be seen as a complex of energies that can be shaped into whatever form the mind conceives. People will learn to harness and work with etheric matter in the same way they learned to work with bricks and mortar.

Telepathic Communication

Those who see etherically will naturally develop the ability to transmit and receive information through the etheric byways, which serve as the transmission lines of telepathic communication. Even today, this ability is widely manifested as more and more realize the power of the mind to communicate with other minds. Many people who live closely together communicate telepathically. Many people find it more and more common that if they merely think of a friend, that friend will contact them out of the blue. Others who act on hunches or intuition are receiving telepathic messages from their guides or picking up general information from the general consciousness. These seeds of telepathy will fully bloom and grow in accuracy as life in the Spiritual Regions develops.

Telepathy can be defined as thought transference between two people or between a person and another intelligent discarnate in different dimension. A thought is sent to a receiver, and the receiver accepts it by forming the atoms necessary to transform the thought into a language that the conscious mind can understand. Telepathy is a natural mode of communication within the etheric realm and has become more pronounced on the earth plane as we approach 2012.

During the initial phase of life in the Spiritual Regions, communications will rely on the remnants of the present wireless or even shortwave systems. These systems will eventually give way to more perfected use of telepathy. This transition is much like the one made from the fax machine to the use of email as the latter's reliability was demonstrated and proven. There will come a time in the near future when telepathic accuracy will reach a level where people will be able to fix the date and place of a meeting mentally and both parties will be there, not by happenstance, but by pre-arranged telepathic arrangement. Later telepathy will constitute a major component in the transference of thought-forms between the etheric and physical planes. It will also serve to link Spiritual Regions spread across the face of the earth during a time when the earth's surface is changing.

Continuity of Consciousness

Continuity of consciousness is defined as a constant and sequential recollection of both the inner and outer worlds. It is the power to be fully aware of all happenings in all spheres and departments of man's being during the entire twenty-four hours of the day.[47] As this ability develops, the brain will be able to register simultaneously reactions of the etheric, astral, and mental bodies at the same time. And if each of these inner bodies is engaged in multi-tasking, the brain will one day be able to register all the activities.

The development of this ability will depend on the extent the astral plane is cleared, for what blocks its present manifestation is the murky state of the lower sub-planes of the astral plane.

Multi-Dimensional Thinking

Continuity of consciousness leads to multi-dimensional thinking. Higher vibrations will eventually challenge the concept of time. What has time done for humanity but keep every thought in a linear pattern? With the concept of time changing into blocks of cyclic unfoldment according to the Law of Synchronicity, linear thinking will give way to multi-dimensional thinking. To complete tasks that advance the soul is what is necessary. Those in the Spiritual Regions will gradually dispense with linear thinking and move onto a multi-dimensional approach that is difficult to describe in words.

As an example, imagine a vast honeycomb of bees, all in their right place, busily doing what needs to be done, instead of ideas lined up along a track or road waiting to be expressed logically as time permits. All thought-forms in the honeycomb are all being expressed and UNDERSTOOD consciously and

---

[47] Ibid., p. 423

simultaneously and thus a multi-dimensional life is taking place.

Or think of a tree and all its branches with thousands of leaves expressing themselves — leaf-by-leaf - all at the same time. Each leaf is part of the tree but the multi-expressiveness of the tree at one time is "the fullness of life therein". Multi-dimensional thinking is something mankind has been searching for millennia, the high-powered computer being the predecessor of this phenomenon.

Words cannot express this way of thinking, but our illustration alludes to a picture you can comprehend today.

Ability to Precipitate

As the human kingdom regains its etheric faculties, it will interact once again with the elemental and angelic kingdoms as it did in Lemuria and on Atlantis. As the veil of astral clutter clears out of the astral plane, angelic beings, fairies, devas, and menehunes will become more visible and we will consciously share life with these two kingdoms. They have always been there, working silently and without due credit for their good works, as the concrete mind of mankind became more and more blind to them. Needless to say with the three kingdoms — human, angelic, and elemental - working together, the breadth, depth, and intelligence of the Spiritual Regions will increase exponentially, and the transitional society will undergo a revolution that will carry it to the doorsteps of the New Golden Age.

Precipitation and the Role of the Elementals

Precipitation is simply thinking of something and producing it materially. In the dense physical world, we must pull out our building tools to shape brick and mortar into a house. In the etheric world, we will use our minds to enlist elementals to build things for us according to our plans. Henry Steel Olcott, the co-founder of the Theosophical Society, reminisced in *Old Diary Leaves* how one night while working with Helena Blavatsky on *Isis Unveiled*, he simply stated how nice it would be to eat some fresh grapes. It was winter and had just snowed. All the stores had already closed in New York. Mme. Blavatsky, with a sly smile on her face, told him to look on the bookshelf behind him, where hanging off one of the shelves were "two large bunches of ripe black Hamburgh grapes" which she had asked the elementals to produce![48]

The Spiritual Regions will by necessity have to be self-sufficient in their basic needs. We expect that adepts in the Spiritual Regions will work with the elemental kingdom to precipitate most of the region's needs in the beginning of life in the Spiritual Regions. As the veil of *maya* dissipates and mankind regains its etheric faculties of perception, we will be able to interact with the elemental kingdom and ask them to precipitate our ideas. In this way, concepts of economics and finance as we know them today will come to an end. Supply will, then, always equal demand.

---

[48] Olcott, Henry Steel, *Old Diary Leaves, Vol. 1*, Adyar, Madras, India: Theosophical Publishing House, 1900, pp. 16-17.

The elemental kingdom works upward, from the tiniest intelligence to cosmic level builders of form. Tiny intelligences create small forms like the petals of a flower, a blade of grass, a dewdrop or a snowflake. More advanced builders can form temples. Teams of these small intelligences create human bodies. Others, such as the nature devas, create mountains and cities, until they finally grow to be Silent Watchers of a planet, a solar system or a galaxy.

How will the elementals relate to mankind again, as they did before the earth was beset with *Maya*? The human being has a mind body that, one day, through the magnetic power of the I AM within, will draw form-making elementals around an idea. Elementals are primarily mental beings, and because mankind also has the ability to work on the mental plane, the two will meet there to create forms.

In addition, man possesses the faculty of feelings and emotions that can add the element of the heart into the mixture before it takes form. This is where mankind's renewed interaction with the angelic realm comes together. Angels exude light and meaning onto form. By drawing in and mixing the human element of the heart with the angelic light of beauty, balance, and colour, mankind will be able to precipitate what it needs and with that extra touch that gives life and beauty to precipitation.

Mankind will learn to use its expanded etheric faculties to cooperate with the elemental and angelic kingdoms to control energy through thought and hold a constructive pattern and design until it is precipitated. We will then enjoy perfection in the nature temples - an apple, a pear, a peach, a grape, as we conceive of it.

The scope of creation thus becomes infinite as each individual creates as need dictates.

The Incoming Race: Natural Etheric Faculties

The five etheric faculties are embedded in the new race, the Sixth Root-Race. Most of the older lightbearers have incarnated in bodies of the seventh or last sub-race of the Fifth Root-Race and must revive these faculties by raising their vibrations. But the more youthful lightbearers who have incarnated in the Sixth Root-Race bodies will find it easier to awaken these faculties.

Post World War II New Race Incarnations

The post-World War II generation of lightbearers who have contributed through their accomplishments and intellectual development will make up the senior lightbearers. Most of these lightbearers chose bodies of the last sub-race of the Fifth Root-Race. These vehicles represent the transition from the Fifth to the Sixth Root-Race in that they retain their penchant for concrete thinking, yet can develop etheric faculties over time. It is usually during their awakening and retrieval of past initiation levels that their etheric abilities become evident.

These Fifth Root-Race incarnations represent the tried and true lightbearers who took part in the original planning for this pralaya centuries ago and who have incarnated over and over during the past eight to ten generations to implement early provisions of the plan. Their most recent incarnations were those of the Theosophical Society, Buddhist monks, Yogis, Sufis, and/or reformers of other traditional religions. In this incarnation, they have taken on the mantle of the technocrat, learning certain fields of expertise of the present civilisation that will carry over into and enhance the post-catastrophic era.

These first tier leaders tend to be metaphysicians as well as experts in their professions. Many are drawn to the ancient occult teachings and may at one time in their lives join one of the traditional religions. By their knowledge of the world and experience in traditional religious practices, they constitute the "civilisation's memory bank" and will play an invaluable role in the Spiritual Regions of reviewing and filtering out that which did not serve mankind from that which still has potential.

Post-1960's New Race Incarnations

The post-1960's wave of new race incarnations are made up of 1) souls on the Path of Initiation or 2) souls from other advanced evolutions. All of these incoming Sixth Root-Race incarnations naturally possess etheric abilities such as clairvoyance, clairaudience and clair-sentience at birth. In addition, souls from the advanced evolutions bear technologies that are not yet known to this civilisation but will be released should they choose to settle in the Spiritual Regions. This knowledge should aid the transitional society to resolve any hint of a carry-over of the most debilitating problems of today's world such as poverty, starvation and disease.

Coming into incarnation with these abilities, however, does not guarantee that these newer lightbearers are on the Path of Initiation. Natural clairvoyance does not make a lightbearer, so like the older lightbearers, they must go through the same probation and acceptance retrieval. There is no short cut. The Masters of Wisdom must determine their commitment to their mission and to service to humanity before they can use them in any position of responsibility. They must be taught and given the choice to serve for the benefit of mankind. Not all the post-1960 group will choose this path as they have been exposed and subject to, like all of humanity, the choices of duality. Those who consciously serve the Spiritual Hierarchy will enhance the team in the Spiritual Regions immensely.

These incarnations are popularly known as the Indigo or Crystal children. Coming into incarnation in the 1960's and 1970's, they have been the target of the Dark Forces and have suffered the most. Some chose parents who nurtured and prepared them for service, others led less fortunate lives. Most struggled in the current education system, which considered them misfits and used medication to force their behaviour into conformity. Some chose the route of substance abuse and many resorted to suicide because of their inability to fit in. Too many have been left to wander aimlessly, searching for meaning.

Despite these hardships, the many who have managed to surmount these challenges will constitute the second tier lightbearers who will be instrumental in shaping the transitional society. They will be the parents of Sixth Root-Race children.

It will be theirs and the elders' duty to teach the new race children how to apply their talents for the good of humanity and in service to the Spiritual

Hierarchy. If not, these talents or abilities will violate the Cosmic Laws of Containment and Abatement. Unleashing these talents without spiritual restraint could sabotage the march to a New Golden Age.

Joining of the Three Kingdoms of Evolution

As Fifth Root-Race thinking became more and more concrete and intellectual, it pushed aside mankind's ability to communicate with the elemental and angelic kingdoms. This deprived us of the richness and radiance of life with these kingdoms. The Master Sanctus Germanus' goal in the New Golden Age is to establish a brotherhood of elementals, angels and mankind. In the Spiritual Regions the three kingdoms - angelic, human and elemental - shall worship together, serve together and walk together on the path.

These kingdoms represent three parallel tracks of evolution under the authority of the Planetary Logos, Sanat Kumara. The angelic kingdom is more advanced than the human kingdom while the human kingdom has more breadth than the elemental intelligences. Elementals are specific task-oriented intelligences that put thoughts into form. As we saw above, these include the devas, nano-intelligences, elves, menehunes and other consciousnesses who will help us build the transitional society.

The angelic kingdom has also continued to serve humanity as virtual unknowns, dishonoured by the concrete mind and relegated to the short Christmas season when they are given recognition. In the Spiritual Regions, angels, seraphims and cherubims will walk with mankind. They exist only to radiate the nature of God, the virtue of God. "They do not labour,

199

they shine!" And with their light, they teach and lead mankind back to the I AM within. Angels perceive mankind only as light and shadow, not as form.

So whereas the consciousness of the elemental is to sacrifice freedom, happiness and joy to enter into the thought pattern developed by man, giving form to that idea by their lives, the consciousness of the angels is to draw divine radiance through the form, giving it life and blessing it. So as astral feelings and emotions dissipate with the astral plane, mankind will no longer react to vast swings on the emotional spectrum, but exude angelic radiance and pure stable feelings.

Angelic emanations, their healing energies and guiding light on matters from the simplest to the most complex concerning life in the Spiritual Regions will have a soothing, stabilizing effect on society. With the presence of and interaction with the angelic realm, what could possibly go wrong? The greater the role the Angelic realm is permitted to play in the transitional society, the greater the chance that mankind will achieve that eon of peace in the New Golden Age.

Touching the Etheric

Mankind's re-activation of five etheric faculties, the incoming new race with its enhanced talents and abilities, and the conscious coexistence with the elemental and angelic kingdoms all support a more etheric existence. In fact, one could characterize the Spiritual Regions by their "in-between-ness" of dimension. The Spiritual Hierarchical structure will extend down into the etheric while the physical plane will reach up to it. Both incarnate and discarnate adepts and lightbearers of the Spiritual Hierarchy straddling these planes will lead the Spiritual Regions' populations to the realization of the Divine Plan that is laid out for each area.

Although much of Spiritual Regional life in the initial years will take place on the dense physical level, lightbearers involved in the planning and decision-making will straddle the two dimensions. If everything goes according to Plan, the transitional society will gradually lose its dense physical nature and operate entirely on the etheric level, and as each new generation takes over, working on the etheric plane will become more and more second nature until the entire transitional society is able to operate primarily on the etheric plane.

As time passes, the transitional society will gradually fade out and the entire New Golden Age civilisation will exist on the etheric. Everything has been meticulously planned over the centuries for this occasion and the intense involvement of the Spiritual Hierarchy, primarily on the etheric, will greatly reduce chaos during this period.

Earth Itself Becomes more Etheric

While this evolution is taking place in the Spiritual Regions, the earth will continue to undergo major physical convulsions and further cleansing of its astral plane. Physical earth itself will appear to shrink as its etheric body takes on more prominence. Over the centuries, physical earth will thus appear to spin faster, creating even higher vibrations and a faster sense of time. On the microcosmic level, the same phenomenon will be observed as our physical bodies become less evident and etheric faculties begin to take on more prominence.

As earth ascends, the vibrations of its etheric plane will increase, which will necessarily affect mankind's etheric bodies. As these ever-higher energies penetrate the dense physical body through the etheric body, the physical body should become lighter and shrink, just as earth's physical body shrinks. It will thus benefit more readily from the inflow of *prana* from the Sun. A New Golden Age, based more on etheric qualities of the body will be revolutionary, compared to the present civilisation.

Interaction with the Spiritual Hierarchy

The acuity of the etheric faculties in the Spiritual Regions will greatly enhance the ability of the populations to communicate with the Spiritual Hierarchy. It also obviates the need of the Masters of the Wisdom to expend a great deal of energy to manifest in dense physical matter. They can take bodies of etheric matter to work at the Hierarchy's centre, Shamballa, on the etheric plane.

Projects undertaken in the Spiritual Regions during the Period of Reconstruction will require close interface with the Spiritual Hierarchy, enhanced by the fact that the majority of the inhabitants will possess these five faculties. We will discuss further the close interaction between the adepts and lightbearers on earth and the Spiritual Hierarchy in Chapter 8.

Shamballa "Returns" to the North Pole

As it becomes clear that the transitional society is progressing into a more etheric existence, lightbearers will be prompted to begin building the thirteenth Spiritual Region, the capital of the New Golden Age. The capital is to be located under Shamballa, and lightbearers from all the Spiritual Regions will decide on the exact location.

Occult lore has speculated that the mystical seat of the Spiritual Hierarchy, Shamballa, is situated either above the Himalayan mountain range or slightly to their north over central Asia. In the present cycle it is estimated that at peak misalignment between the two axes, Shamballa was located as far off as the northern tips of the Himalayas instead of above the North Pole. As the earth has already begun shifting back to alignment with its etheric double, Shamballa's location over the centuries also seems to be shifting.

When earth's poles have finally aligned with those etheric, Shamballa should be located above what is today the North Pole. At this point, another era of peak enlightenment on earth will open up a New Golden Age of contact between Shamballa and the earth plane, especially the Spiritual Regions.

CHAPTER 8

Period of Reconstruction III

Functioning of the Transitional Society

The basic structure of the transitional society will be comprised of 1) a minimal governing hierarchy and 2) a vast free sector of activity where residents have full freedom to live as they please. The whole society will come under cosmic law.

Such a society will serve as a model for the coming New Golden Age. However, we can only indicate the basic framework within which it will operate. How it will ultimately evolve will be left to the infinite creativity of the Spiritual Regions' inhabitants. In the previous chapter we have indicated that mankind will regain etheric abilities that will profoundly affect the transitional society's functions. So we can only project a provisional vision as its entire future and shape rests in the hands of the residents. The Spiritual Hierarchy can only guide, for the principle of free will still be in force during the New Golden Age.

Governing Structure: Principle of Hierarchy in Action

Those who move to the Spiritual Regions will experience an active interaction with the Spiritual Hierarchy, where Its adepts have been placed as an extension of Its structure on the earth plane. We indicated previously that ancient secret societies linked to the Brotherhood of Light or Spiritual Hierarchy have already been activated, and that adepts of these societies are now moving into the Spiritual Regions in preparation for population displacements. These adepts, appearing like ordinary citizens of the region, will work quietly and without fanfare with the lightbearers and their followers to prepare the Spiritual Regions to receive and settle those moving up from the lowlands.

The governing structure in the Spiritual Regions will mirror that of the Hierarchy, which is essentially a consultative, centralized hierarchical structure. While this structure implies top down governance, its main activities and movements promote upward mobility, i.e. spiritual development.

Even groups will be ranked in the hierarchical order and their internal organisation will also follow the same hierarchical principles that comprise the Order of the Universe.

In such a Hierarchy there is always one who is on a higher rung, protecting and overseeing the welfare of those on lower rungs. So at any level of the hierarchy, the hierarch benevolently cares for and educates those below — never oppressive, sometimes strict, yet applying the principle of love with careful guidance — all of which promotes the evolution of a lower rung to the higher rungs. Everyone is a hierarch, and everyone is under a hierarch.

The upward movement promotes Soul Liberation, the prime *raison d'être* of the Hierarchy on our planet. This same principle will apply to all group activity, large and small. All organizations and their leadership hierarchy, no matter what the activity, should in some way promote Soul Liberation, and this liberation implies the movement up the hierarchical ladder.

One of the great fears that remains with today's lightbearer is the oppressive characteristics that hierarchy can or has taken during the present era. Hierarchy, as interpreted on the earth plane, has resulted in some of the most oppressive dictatorial and monarchical regimes that mankind has ever invented. Modern history records hierarchical dictatorial regimes countries as the Soviet Union and China, not to mention the ruthless petty dictatorships in South America, Africa and Asia. Even democratically elected structures worldwide have been corrupted to the point that they now override their peoples' voice to wage wars and oppress. Alternative horizontal or flat organizational structures, with which mankind experimented to overcome the oppressive nature of monarchies or dictatorships, have withered, unsuccessful.

So democratically-minded people who fear the return of a dictatorial theocratic hierarchy do so based on the miserable experiences in mankind's history. So here we must call attention to the cosmic laws outlined above. The Laws of Abandonment and Reverse Motion apply in this instance. There is a need to break with dysfunctional experiences of the past to allow for the full expression of a time-honoured divine structure to take root.

The Governing Hierarchy of the Spiritual Regions

Led by the principle that the lightest governing structure is best for a society whose goal is to foster Soul Liberation, the following governmental structure would apply to the Spiritual Regions, subject to the people's approval:

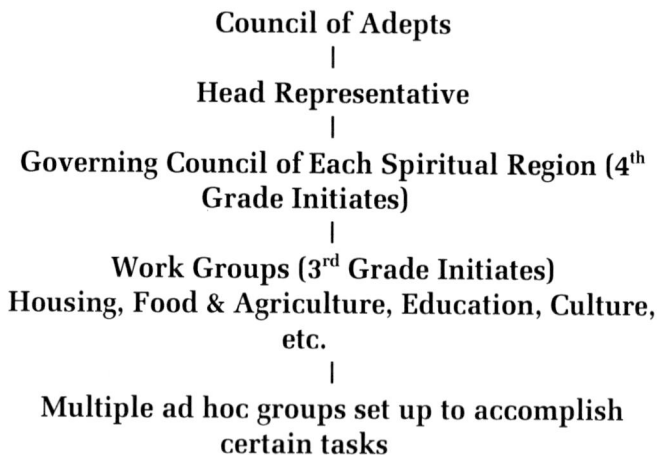

Council of Adepts
|
Head Representative
|
Governing Council of Each Spiritual Region (4ᵗʰ Grade Initiates)
|
Work Groups (3ʳᵈ Grade Initiates)
Housing, Food & Agriculture, Education, Culture, etc.
|
Multiple ad hoc groups set up to accomplish certain tasks

Council of Adepts

The Council of Adepts will be made up of spiritual adepts currently working on the earth plane. These adepts are to be identified by the Master Sanctus Germanus and will represent the Spiritual Hierarchy on earth. The Council of Adepts will operate like an elders' council to give advice and insight to Spiritual Regions on all matters.

The Council of Adepts will guide the establishment of all Spiritual Regions at their inception. Once the hierarchy for each Spiritual Region is established, the Council will be concerned primarily with the relations between Spiritual Regions, which may include anything from trade to cultural exchanges. It will also appoint the Head Representative for each Region and he or she will be able to consult the Council for advice concerning any decisions to be made.

The Council will eventually function out of the New Golden Age capital, which will be constructed North of Canada or on Greenland, depending on what transpires during the intervening years. The capital will be located under the etheric city of Shamballa.

Like all organizations or groups on the earth plane, there will be a counterpart Council in the etheric zone at work in concert with that on earth, but it is, of course, the earthly Council that will have the last word. Members of the Council of Adepts will demonstrate their ease in straddling both planes and will communicate freely with their etheric counterparts as equal colleagues acting from different perspectives.

Communications between the Council and its etheric counterpart will occur via telepathy. Proceedings will be open to the public through advanced lightbearers serving as telepathic interpreters. Telepathy will eventually become the sole mode of communication as it guarantees openness in government.

As the Council's functions increase over time due to increased interaction between Spiritual Regions, its future administrative form will be based on the highest principles of hierarchical organization as practiced by the Spiritual Hierarchy. There will be no bureaucracies.

The Head Representative of the Spiritual Region

The Hierarchy and the Council of Adepts will appoint a Head Representative to lead each Spiritual Region. The Head Representative will most likely be a Master-level Adept, manifesting in both masculine or feminine forms, from the regional branch of the Brotherhood of Light. [49]

Although appearing in the flesh for this function, the Head Representative will most likely be an immortal capable of manifesting in and out of the physical body at will and when necessary. This Master Adept will serve as the ultimate earthly authority in the Spiritual Region, and will utter the last word in any major decision concerning the Spiritual Region. His or Her mandate will be given by the Spiritual Hierarchy, assuring purity of governance.

While the Head Representative functions as the moral and spiritual head, daily operational decisions

---

[49] The Brotherhood of Light has regional branches throughout the world, e.g. the Luxor, Egypt Branch, South American Branch and the North American Branch to name a few.

will be relegated to the Governing Council of each Region. If deadlocked on any issue, the Head Representative will cast the tie-breaking vote.

Even though it represents a higher authority, the Council of Adepts cannot override any decisions taken by the Head Representative and Spiritual Regions' Governing Councils as each region must be responsible for its own decisions.

The Head Representative represents, and guarantees total transparency to, all the people of the Spiritual Region, since no secrets or ulterior motives among all levels of leadership will be kept from the public, due to increasing mental abilities and clairvoyance.

Governing Council of the Spiritual Region

A governing council will lead the Spiritual Regions' everyday operations. Third and fourth initiate level lightbearers of the Spiritual Hierarchy will serve on the Governing Councils.

The Head Representative will appoint to the Governing Council members out of a pool of volunteers according to their level of spiritual development, as meticulously recorded in the Hall of Records in Shamballa. Popularity is not a criterion. Council members will represent every walk of life. They will embody experience, earthly knowledge, and an ability to practice White Magic. They will possess all the basic faculties of etheric sight, clairvoyance, telepathic powers, continuity of consciousness, and precipitation, to enable active interaction with their etheric counterparts from the Spiritual Hierarchy, who will comment and advise them without overriding their inherent rights of free will.

Governing Councils will function quite differently from local governments today. First, there will be a general homogeneity among members in line with the Law of Attraction. Although differences will exist, they will not result in separate, warring interest groups. Differences, rather than being dichotomous, will be seen as another facet of an issue, enhancing it with substance and depth. Second, the significant population reduction will ease stress on governing structures, enabling them to be streamlined - a far cry from the groaning bureaucracies we see on earth today. Third, and most importantly, the five developed etheric faculties will guarantee openness.

Lightbearers will bring their hard-won experience to the discussion table in all different fields, while their etheric counterparts will also contribute their ageless perspective and practical experience gained from past incarnations. Communication between the two planes will be perfected as both constituents meet straddling the two dimensions.

To assure inter-dimensional communication in the Governing Council, a group of telepathic sensitives and advanced spiritual adepts will be responsible for maintaining telepathy between Spiritual Regions. They will develop methods to increase the accuracy of messages between groups.

Thus, telepathic communication will result in a whole new "open" society heretofore unseen. It will revolutionize governance and eliminate politics, because no secrets can be kept from the governed. This faculty alone will revolutionize society as we know it today and help create the much-promised Golden Age.

Ad Hoc Task Groups Under the Governing Council

Today, businesses, churches, charitable institutions and the like come together in a setting that promotes division. The accepted norm dictates that there are constant forces at work to break up groups—disagreements, differing goals (usually selfish ones)—a general tug and pull so that each group loses its dynamism and, in the event it stays together, reaches the lowest common denominator equal to what we see in bureaucracies — a general numbness and mediocrity of purpose and action with excellence and innovation restricted by inertia and fear. The cosmic Law of Attraction will determine membership in a Spiritual Region group, and much of the conflict and disagreement that is characteristic of present-day group activity will be minimized or eliminated.

Survivors emerging from a decade of initial earth changes will have learned a monumental lesson of group cooperation, for their survival will have depended on group cooperation. The "trauma" will break the mindset of rugged individualism in favour of shared action. Even before arriving in the Spiritual Regions, it is likely that small groups of lightbearers will already have formed. During their journeys, strong bonding will have formed in each group. Being led to the Spiritual Regions without access to conventional communications, many survivors will have relied on telepathic communication through etheric channels to reach their destination.

In the transitional society, groups and organizations under the governing hierarchy will be task-driven. Once the task has been completed, the group will disband, eliminating the need for multi-layered bureaucracies that linger and drain.

No matter what the functional purpose of a group, its activity must contribute in some way to the ultimate goal of the Spiritual Region; Soul Liberation. This goal will bind all activities in the Region so that coherence exists between the transitional society's activities.

All groups will have counterparts in the etheric dimension. Etheric ashrams under certain Masters will be the basis of group formation on the earth plane. Some members may chose to take etheric forms on the etheric plane in order to communicate better with their fellows on the physical plane. This mix of etheric and physical members in each group will characterize all group formations in the Spiritual Regions. If a group of healers forms in the Spiritual Region, experienced healers from the higher dimensions will join them on the etheric plane. If a group of engineers forms to build a structure, spirit engineers will cooperate.

Transitional Nature of the Governing Structure

In this system of hierarchical governance, from the Council of Adepts to the Spiritual Region Governing Council and task groups, an enlightened view of hierarchy will be required. When seen as extensions of the Spiritual Hierarchy into the etheric and physical planes, they can never be oppressive, for they only promote upward movement.

Order will need to be established, initially, by the strong presence of members of the Hierarchy. Given the potential chaos of the period, intense spiritual nurturing will be necessary to restore order after the initial destructive stage of the pralaya. All three levels of governance will benefit from this guidance as it pours down from their etheric plane counterparts of the Spiritual Hierarchy.

As Regional leaders gain confidence and a foothold on their functions, more and more responsibility will fall upon the following generations as the Masters and adepts gradually withdraw and allow the upward momentum of initiation to feed the governing ranks. It is conceivable that the Head Representative would one day come from the ranks of the earthly Fourth level lightbearers.

But it is also possible that the earthly leaders may tire or plot to block the influence of their etheric counterparts and strike out on their own. This has happened in past civilisations as society indulges in both sensual and selfish enterprises. In this case, etheric counterparts will withdraw and allow mankind's free will to function.

Qualifications of the Governing Leaders

The Head Representatives of the Spiritual Regions will be chosen from among two sorts: 1) Masters who have taken on physical bodies and worked for centuries on the earth plane and 2) Masters who have been working with lightbearers from the mental plane on this pralaya and who will take on semi-physical-etheric vehicles to operate in the Spiritual Regions.

Other leaders in the Spiritual Region Governing Council and Ad Hoc task groups will come from the ranks of Fourth and Third level initiates/lightbearers. The criteria for leadership will come from their knowledge of a certain field of expertise and their mastery of White Magic. Leadership in the Spiritual Regions will be re-defined, putting one's spiritual qualifications ahead of expertise. The combination will be powerful, especially when aligned with the goals of the Divine Plan.

Fourth Level Initiate-Lightbearers in Incarnation[50]

Many Fourth level initiates have sacrificed their further evolution on the spiritual planes to come back to work for humanity as lightbearers during this pralaya. These initiate-lightbearers will fill the ranks of the Governing Council. Their journey to this point could be described as follows:

> The life of the man who takes the fourth initiation, or the Crucifixion, is usually one of great sacrifice and suffering. It is the life of the man who makes the Great Renunciation, and even exoterically it is seen to be strenuous, hard, and painful. He has laid all, even his perfected personality, upon the altar of sacrifice, and stands bereft of all. All is renounced, friends, money, reputation, character, standing in the world, family, and even life itself.[51]

Many of these renunciates can be found among the mystics in the traditional religions of the world,

---

[50] See Alice A. Bailey's *Initiation Human and Solar*, New York: Lucis Trust and C.W. Leadbeater's *The Masters and the Path*, Adyar: Theosophical Publishing House.

[51] Bailey, Alice A. *Initiation Human and Solar*, p. 90.

however there are also many fourth level initiates who lead renunciate lives in a non-religious context. They can be found in almost all walks of life, often camouflaged as those quiet workers of light tucked away in the halls of power and influence. Those who hold high positions in government and finance outwardly appear like their colleagues of the Dark Forces, but inwardly they do much to moderate the evil being perpetrated. Such is their sacrifice and suffering as they live day to day on the brink of crucifixion! As the Dark Forces are defeated, these initiate-lightbearers will emerge triumphant to lead with a perspective that is worldly-wise whilst true to the spiritual principles of the Divine Plan. They will speak of the past with the authority of experience and trial. And they will draw on this experience to carry over into the New Golden Age that part of mankind's evolution which is good and positive.

Once in the Spiritual Regions, these fourth level initiate-lightbearers will liaise between their corresponding ashrams in the Spiritual Hierarchy and the earth plane and as leaders. Prepared to work both on the etheric and physical planes before going to the Spiritual Regions, initiate-lightbearers will insure that the hierarchy's plans and suggestions are clearly articulated to the safe area populations.

Third Level Initiate-Lightbearers in Incarnation

Third level lightbearers permeate every field of worldly endeavour, mastering the sciences, economics, politics, business, banking, finance etc. Some even work as securities' and stock brokers. These are the odd ones who silently feel they are not part of the corporate world or not part of their scientific community but still practice or contribute to their particular field of endeavour. Yet, most feel a gnawing sense that there is more to life. Their search first takes them into a passing and futile search for truth in the traditional churches and temples.

Their feeling of detachment arises from the fact that their Higher Selves are in tune with the higher dimensions during sleep hours while during their conscious hours, they are very much aware of something greater than themselves. This is where their careers conflict with their hearts. Many suffer silently yet excel within the confines of human organizations until they receive the signal from the hallowed halls of the upper dimensions that it is time to separate from their careers and start a new cycle. They are the ripe fruit ready for harvest, prepared in every field of endeavour for the future divine unfoldment during the period of reconstruction: an Army of Lightbearers, lightbearers in expertise as the great plan unfolds.

At the third initiation, sometimes called the Transfiguration, the entire personality is flooded with light from above. It is only after this initiation that the Monad is definitely guiding the personality. The initiate-lightbearer is in a position at all times to recognize the other members of the Spiritual Hierarchy, and his or her psychic faculties are stimulated by the vivification of the *head centres.* Spiritual intuition, clairaudience and clairvoyance are awakened when the body is pure, the astral body stable and the mental body under control. At this point the initiate is ready to use wisely the psychic faculties for the helping of the race.[52]

---

[52] Ibid., p. 87

In the Spiritual Regions the third level initiate-lightbearer will fill all leadership positions, either in the Governing Hierarchy or in the Free Sector. By this time they will carry knowledge, both esoteric and worldly, that will enable them to lead groups and projects. They will organize and see to the daily functioning of local councils and groups. These are the equivalent of the esoteric "technocrat" who can work to implement projects both from the physical and the etheric planes.

First and Second Level Lightbearers

There are a great number of these initiate-lightbearers who feel a call from within yet respond more to the call from without. Most struggle with the problems posed by the dense physical body and a personality that is burdened with self-doubt, mental rationalization, and astral thrills and confusion, yet deep down they know that "something" is coming. These are the "fence sitters", the uncommitted who pose endless questions hoping to find the answer they want to hear--primarily that "everything is going to be alright." If they choose to join life in the Spiritual Regions, their initiation process will accelerate, and they may find themselves handling more than one initiation in a lifetime. For this to happen requires commitment to the Plan, not in words but in action, and this is what may hinder further progress. Sometimes they require commitment on their terms, comfortable and non-earth-shaking. But in the post-Great Floods era, they will either be jolted into commitment or pass from the earth with the others.

The Free Sector

All other residents on all planes who are not engaged in the governing hierarchy will be free to live as they choose. They can form learning institutions, provide a multitude of services for one another, form relationships with past friends and enemies, form group activities of the entire range of human endeavour---a full life. This will be the Free Sector.

Many of the leaders in the Free Sector will come from the ranks of the third level initiate-lightbearers.

Let us project how the Free Section in the transitional society might look by examining it from our traditional categories of the economy, health, education, and spiritual life:

1. The Economy: Goods, Services and Precipitation

In the transitional society many will naturally volunteer their services to build what is needed for the common good. If a road, school, or any project for common good of the society needs to be built, architects, engineers, construction-savvy personnel and builders will volunteer their services.

Residents in the Spiritual Regions will have the opportunity to re-evaluate what they need as opposed to what they desire. The cleansing of the astral plane and individual astral bodies will reduce what is desired to the essentials. Over-consumption will no longer burden society and the "urge to shop" will be transformed into an urge to serve. People will meet their needs through the abundance of resources available to them in the Spiritual Regions, but at the same time, their needs will be very much reduced. For instance, they will eat less, feeding on the new inflow of *prana* rather than food. And as the transitional society advances, residents will gain the ability to precipitate the basics from etheric matter.

Supply through Precipitation

During the initial period in the Spiritual Regions, adepts of the Hierarchy will feed the people much like the Master Jesus fed the multitudes --through precipitation. They will set the example of what is to come. And through education and spiritual development and the recognition of the form-making role of the elementals, all members of the transitional society will learn to precipitate basic needs.

Precipitation is giving form to thought. In the Spiritual Regions we will give form to thought through both dense and etheric matter. Atoms, a form of dense matter, surround a thought-form and a solid object is created. A thought in an engineer's mind eventually becomes an automobile. Another thought in a designer's mind becomes a dress. In our world, thoughts eventually precipitate in dense matter.

Thoughts can also manifest through etheric matter; in fact most thoughts streaming from the soul exist first in the etheric before manifesting in dense matter. One advantage of etheric thought forms is that they can be telepathically transmitted from one location to the other. One day it will be common to receive both telepathic messages and objects through the etheric by-ways. As etheric vision becomes more and more acute, we will see and benefit from etheric materializations and eventually dispense with the dense material world. However, in the transitional society there will be a mix of the precipitated and the material before full etheric precipitation is recognized.

When everyone develops the ability to precipitate, it will be the ultimate solution to all want. Even today, many lightbearers who may be struggling financially may suddenly find resources at their disposal: an inheritance, a good investment, and even money that appears out of nowhere. It is not uncommon in our world to experience precipitation, and we will benefit from this phenomenon more and more as White Magicians work to alleviate suffering during the economic depression.

As precipitation becomes more prevalent, it will open the floodgates of real creativity. Individuals will be able to create what their souls want to manifest. What one creates might delight another and vice versa; there we would plant a seed for exchange. Precipitation is the ultimate of individual creativity. No more will mankind be controlled by mass fashions and fads. The individual's creativity will be returned to the individual soul. This is part of Soul Liberation.

Exchange and Gold

Money has been the most important factor of this civilisation—perhaps the most important. As a medium of exchange it was a means of easing the burden of goods transfer in a barter system. But even given the best solutions, mankind has a way of turning such innovations to selfish ends. Mankind has not yet learned the lesson of money and for this reason, money will continue to be used well into the transitional society.

The current system of national fiat paper currencies is barrelling down the road to self-destruction because there is nothing behind them bar political rhetoric. All currencies are irredeemable in that there is no gold or silver to back them. Once people see the whole paper system for what it is - paper - people will revert to gold and silver as a medium of exchange.

People will meet their needs through exchange or barter. Gold and silver coins will be used to even out the exchange or serve as money to purchase assets such as building tools, supplies, and materials. So we can expect gold and silver as money to carry over into the Spiritual Regions after the Great Floods, most importantly to even out barter exchanges and purchase machinery or supplies for projects.

Many elevated cities in the world will survive the Great Floods and resort to gold and silver as universal money. Rather than national paper currencies, people will trade on the basis of grams or ounces of gold or silver, no matter where it comes from and in what form.

With means as yet unknown to us, the Spiritual Hierarchy will release gold into the economies of the Spiritual Regions. Gold has been hoarded for millennia, and supply is plentiful on the earth - the Dark Forces have just hidden and monopolized it. The release of these great quantities of gold into full circulation will enable a stable, non-inflation/deflation prone economy to thrive.

The gold and silver system will be used during the transitional society's initial period but as mankind masters precipitation, manifestation will take over: think and therefore it will be. But to transit from a monetary system to one of precipitation, we must first transit through barter-gold-silver exchange.

Banks Not Needed

Since we must live with money until we learn to use it properly to solve mankind's problems, it must be taken out of the hands of any central control—and that means any community, city, national, or international control. This has been the root of the money problem today. The current monetary system is controlled by so few people. Paper money took away control from the individual. Electronic money has been even more ephemeral. It comes and goes---mainly goes-- at the speed of light at night!

The Dark Forces created a banking system based on fractional reserves. Bank can lend out an amount of paper money equal to ten times more than the value of its gold holdings. This is how bankers got so rich--by lending out worthless, irredeemable paper money *at interest.* Banks, in essence, use your money to make more money for themselves and through more complex paper transactions involving more paper (i.e. stocks and bonds), they have created stock markets, derivative and bond markets, and other financial instruments. The collapse of this house of cards is the reason for the economic depression of 2007.

In the Spiritual Regions the management of money energy will revert to individual control. However, if banks do form, they will constitute primarily places of safe storage. If a bank exists only for the storage of a person's savings, the use of that money remains solely in the hands of its owner, not of the storage facility or bank. Then a person who is imbued with a sense of service and of cosmic law can use this money or gold for that which promotes directly or indirectly Soul Liberation. The connection of an individual's accumulation of money energy to his or her knowledge of cosmic laws will be very important to assure the right and proper use of money. The proper use of money is a lesson mankind has yet to master and will constitute a primal prerequisite to entering the New Golden Age.

2. Health and Dis-Ease and Telepathic Healing

In the years leading up to the Great Floods, the Dark Forces will resort to manufactured disease in the form of pandemics in an attempt to drag as much of humanity down as they are defeated. Manufactured diseases and pandemics are used politically to control and create a dependence on state institution and cow people into submission. We cite AIDS and Avian Flu as prime examples of manufactured diseases designed to incite fear, panic and kill millions. Many latter day germ warfare tactics will use carriers of the animal kingdom — such as insects — to transmit these diseases around the world. The extent to which the Dark Forces succeed in its mass pandemic killings is as yet unknown, but we can at least predict that they will lose at the end of this diabolical tactic.

Pollution has been the cause of multiple mutations of "good" bacteria into harmful ones while the human body loses its resistance to microbes due to faulty diet and stressful conditions. Is it no wonder the earth needs to flood her surface with the sea's cleansing waters? How brine of various strengths will be applied to this cleanup is a matter of systematic and intelligent application and not, as man would suspect, random destruction. So the cleansing of those areas infested with disease — either through the drying and parching powers of the Sun or the cleansing of brine - will be aimed at these insalubrious areas.

Thus we see that the two main sources of today's diseases will be eliminated in the Spiritual Regions, and the nature of disease will move more into the realm of mental challenges. Those who survive these difficult times will do so because their vibrations have increased to the point that disease cannot touch or harm them. It is a matter of vibration, not the immune system.

Nature of Disease in the Transitional Society

During the transitional society, dis-ease will result more from psychological issues than from organic sources. The carryover dis-eases will affect survivors more than their offspring, for in the future mankind will be more or less free from organic disease.

Surviving populations in the Spiritual Regions and their surrounding areas will experience maladies due primarily to their adjusting to higher vibrations. Since 2000, higher vibrations and acceleration of time have pushed humanity to the point of insanity. Among those who go to the Spiritual Regions, even higher vibrational adjustments will be required, and as the dense physical form lets go of layer after layer of dense atoms, this process will not be without pain and discomfort. There will be unease due to the constant detoxification the body vehicle must carry out as it rises in vibration. All must undergo this bodily transition. Much of what we foresee coming to the surface in the form of detoxification will be the deep traumas associated with life's upheavals during the earth changes.

Such major adjustments to the body vehicle will take place at a time when level-headedness and accurate acumen are most needed. Those adjusting will experience disorientation, a feeling of being, but not really being -- much like a bad case of jetlag. Any residual psychological issues that have managed to stay within the lower mental and astral/emotional bodies will be summarily forced to the surface during this period, and the care and love of group members will be beneficial to recuperation.

Gradually, as the surviving population adjusts to the higher vibrations, disease, as we know it today will disappear, and dis-ease will take the form of resistance or backlash to new concepts and teachings of the Ancient Wisdom. Mental resistance to new teachings of the Ancient Wisdom that are meant to provoke change for the better will cause stress that will manifest eventually as unwanted physical dis-ease. The struggles and challenges of evolution never end. . . such is what we experience in our dimension.

Inner Struggle with Duality

The journey from our lower emotional (lower astral) to our mental bodies will bring out lower emotional problems similar to those we deal with today. However, the journey from the higher astral to the mental body that touches the higher spiritual self brings its own type of problems, and if misdirected, can cause symptoms resembling mental insanity. Most of the residents in the Spiritual Regions will encounter this type of adjustment.

The polarity that characterizes our illusory life on earth today provides moral choice through the battle of opposites. The impetus of good to self-express keeps the battle with evil going, making life challenging and interesting on this plane. Will the earth changes obviate this situation of duality? The answer is no. The struggle within dense and etheric matter will continue, but more internally. The internal battle could be perceived as someone conversing with himself, joining the ranks of the insane.

Battles and struggles will occur within. Your right to choose among alternatives will continue and what you choose shall be your path to wisdom. And yes, sometimes your choice may not be appropriate, but you will nonetheless be given many more chances to choose from that which will fit your mental needs perfectly.

Choices, choices, choices. How lucky you are! The differences will be oh, so subtle, and the mental body must be, oh, so acute to discern the differences and advantages. And will the emotions come into play? Why, yes, but more different and higher emotions than you can imagine. Ah, those sublime, provocative thoughts somewhat like what beautiful works of art will evoke. And those well-thought-out discourses you hear and the plays and the music—all these will contain such subtle thought-forms that will either retard or advance your spiritual ascension.[53]

Meditation and education can resolve this battle, which consists of peeling off the physical in favour of the etheric. You must consciously contend with two bodies at the same time. Many will have won this battle before 2012 but the vast majority of lightbearers who plan to enter the reconstruction phase in the Spiritual Regions must face this struggle ahead. The challenge never ends but each time you reach a plateau, there is a heaven to behold, making the struggle all the more worthwhile.

Did you think your lessons would end in the New Golden Age? They never end, but grow more and more subtle, requiring razor sharp spiritual discernment, discernment of the sort that does not exist in this dimension. As the grosser elements recede from human consciousness, you will touch the hem of this subtlety as the years approach the big changes.

And even during the cataclysms, you will be treated to light views of what is going on, so that the change will take on a new meaning, a new perception not ever seen by present mankind. And each time this new perception is understood, physical changes will take place in your body vehicle. But you'll adjust so that you can carry out your purpose. The grosser elements of humankind have so weighed down your thinking and have blotted out this level of perception. It shall be restored in full glory and you will understand that sweetness that is of Spirit, and this sweetness is what you will call health.[54]

---

[53] Sanctus Germanus through the Amanuensis
[54] Ibid.

Telepathic Healing Modalities

It is at this critical juncture that the Planetary Logos —the Ancient of Days— who has seen and experienced countless pralayas, has provided mankind with healing energies that can be telepathically transmitted or diverted to those under stress by trained practitioners. Healing was a great part of the Master Jesus' mission on earth, and we are told that His ability to heal came directly from the Planetary Logos. [55] So spiritual healing in its most effective form is actually the response of dense or etheric matter to the highest vibrational and finest etheric energy. This energy must come from sources higher than the etheric plane and contain the direct intention of healing of anything that does not conform to cosmic law.

Telepathic healing, while alleviating discomfort, is the clarion call to draw others into the bosom of spirit. It is a tool of White Magic to demonstrate liberation from the limitations of the physical vehicle. The most effective spiritual healings will occur in those pursuing the Path of Initiation. Spiritual healing, thus, has a purpose: it unblocks obstacles to Soul Liberation.

Lightbearers pursuing their purpose and mission in the Divine Plan will naturally acquire healing abilities and work to assuage fellow lightbearers on the Path, especially during this period of vibrational adjustment. Those without any conscious interest in pursuing the Path will observe such healings and marvel at them. In this sense, healing is a clarion call, a reminder to the general population that healing is

---

[55] Master Serapis Bey, Mystery School Teachings, Sanctus Germanus Foundation.

part of the Path. Otherwise, the general population should seek alternative help in the medical and alternative medicine fields.

3. Education in the Spiritual Regions

Education is key in turning the human mindset toward cosmic law. It is the one function in the Free Sector that the Head Representative will guide directly. We do not foresee a school system per se, but education will spring out of individual or group initiatives in the Free Sector. Not being restricted to classrooms, education will be an ongoing process of interpenetration between dimensions for all inhabitants of the Spiritual Regions. As each lightbearer masters the etheric faculties and thus achieves control over life on the physical and etheric planes, he or she will see members of their etheric ashram standing ready to share information from any level or dimension.

Education and training in the initial years will emphasize techniques for and reinforcement of the five etheric faculties for sharper etheric vision, telepathy, consciousness continuity, multi-dimensional thinking, and precipitation.

Telepathy will play a fundamental role in the dissemination of teachings in the Spiritual Regions. Education will occur wherever a person is or whenever a person desires because it will be available telepathically. Telepathic instruction, much like online education, will thus revolutionize the concept of schools and the heavy infrastructure that is associated with them, and put all students in direct *rapport* with the Masters in charge of teaching. Within an atmosphere that will have been cleansed of the present day astral negativity, the ability to learn from the great teachers of the Christ Office in Shamballa through telepathy will have an immeasurable impact on the individual and society. The teacher will transmit instantly discernable knowledge while the receptive student can give instant feedback about the extent to which this knowledge has taken root, been accepted or rejected. The practises of keeping secrets and hiding ignorance will be better exposed. With telepathic learning, there will be more reliance on oral transmission and review of what has been telepathically conveyed and less dependence on book learning in order that the principles remain alive for practice and review and not merely codified for storage in dusty tomes.

Education of the New Race

Education should consider the talents and abilities that the new race children possess: clairvoyance, clairaudience, clairsentience, etheric vision of the physical eye, continuity of consciousness, telepathy, and the potential to manifest. Tooled with these abilities, these young ones will be given the same earthly choices that will lead them onto the Path or not, but none of these abilities will guarantee their Path of Initiation as this will remain their choice. The super-talented pianist is presented here with the same choices as the day labourer, the clairvoyant as the non-clairvoyant. Clairvoyance is not synonymous with spirituality and one's choice to tread the Path. In fact it complicates the choice, for no longer will the choice be made on blind faith, but with a greater awareness of the different dimensions in which one resides.

The new race will, paradoxically, come to earth through the birth channels of Fifth Root-Race bodies. Therefore there is a need for the Fifth Root-Race to nurture the incoming Sixth Root-Race and at the same time the Sixth Root-Race needs to reform its nurturer. Herein lies the requirement for the new education, one in which mutual respect is required. No longer should "the taught" be under the dominance of the teacher, for the teacher must draw inspiration from "the taught." Yet the world with which these children will deal will involve a vaster dimension than the previous root- race and thus a wider range of conscious choices.

In the Spiritual Regions, these children will face choices that are not tangible to the five senses. It will be easy for them to play on the astral playground without supervision, and they are likely to be misled if they are not taught discipline and discrimination from an early age. Their other bodies -- etheric, astral, and mental -- will be fully activated, adding the need for education that will address the multidimensional aspects of their whole personalities.

The pitfalls are plenty on the astral plane, but if the supervisor cannot see for himself the temptations resident on that plane, how then is he or she going to teach the new race child the necessary discrimination? The answer to this is easy. As above so below. Mental discrimination learned in concrete and abstract thinking is the way, and if well taught even from the point of view of the Fifth Root-Race concrete thinkers, it will serve the children on the astral playgrounds as well, for what is wrong on the physical is wrong on the astral.

So children must be taught discipline and discrimination, when to use their faculties to help society and when it is not appropriate to use them. A clairvoyant child could easily conclude he/she is insane in this world, as he sees that which the others or his "superiors" cannot. But the new race could also use these faculties to run rings around the Fifth Root-Race in an immoral way. In the same way, responsible use of clairvoyance has yet to be achieved by the earlier incarnations of the Sixth Root-Race, as in many instances these faculties have either been suppressed or used in lower psychism.

The worst that an educational program could do would be to suppress these new faculties and remould the young minds into concrete thinking. They must be both firmly rooted in intellectual development and at the same time open to the vast possibilities and inspiration coming from the higher planes. When these faculties are applied to humanity's problems, we can expect creative solutions, for just as we have previously cited possible pitfalls on the astral plane, we also see the infinite possibilities emanating from these children who are able to access and gain inspiration from the highest ideas coming to them from the higher planes. Their use as conduits for creative thought-forms emanating from the Spiritual Hierarchy should be deemed a primary function of these children.

The consciousness of gender should no longer grip the new race children, for they represent an inherent blending and balance of the masculine and feminine. The issue of one sex preying on the other will be less of a problem than in the Fifth Root-Race world. Sixth Root-Race children represent the beginnings of that re-merging and rebalancing of the masculine and feminine and will appear as fairly androgynous or cross-sexual experiences. This interchange of sensuality should not be seen from the point of view of traditional morality but from the viewpoint that such rebalancing can only contribute to peace on earth.

The unisex movement is a superficial example of the tendencies of the new race. Unisex education probes deeper into the inherent equilibrium of the soul or higher Self. When this is recognized in all thought-forms, and not misinterpreted as either masculine or feminine, the war of the sexes will be quelled and the resulting peace in human relationships will again be re-established.[56]

So education in the Spiritual Regions is not just about shaping "good citizens", but also about opening the new race children to the Path of Initiation, which must be "implied" throughout the curriculum, though not explicitly expressed. If this approach is taken, all of the social concerns and adaptability of these innate abilities will fall into place and benefit the reconstruction period.

If educators in the Spiritual Regions approach this challenge from the causal body or Higher Self, they will be able to see education from the highest vantage point and address all the bodies that function together on the earth plane. The etheric counterpart committee will communicate its ideas from an even higher vantage point to its counterpart on earth, and through this cooperation, elaborate modalities that will address

---

[56] Master Kuthumi through the Amanuensis, May, 2006

the multifaceted and multidimensional aspects of a new approach to education.

"Seek and ye shall find" will be the working principle between the education committee and its etheric counterpart, and the choices made in the Spiritual Regions will come from the highest effort and reflect the light that shines down on the New Golden Age. We begin the ascension with the vital element of the new society--education--which is one of the chief means of Soul Liberation.

The basis of this give-and-take is brotherhood. This or sisterhood, if you wish, should permeate the whole educational concept for the New Golden Age. We introduced the concept of Hierarchy where in certain instances the student may be the Hierarch. The humility with which an educator approaches a student has at its root LOVE.

The extraordinary abilities of the new race are not that extraordinary and must be seen as the process by which mankind will regain its inherent faculties so obscured by the thought forms of past ages. With intelligence firmly positioned in dense matter, the ever-evolving challenge is now to refine that density. What we call "gifts" of clairvoyance, clairaudience, and clairsentience, coupled with the ability to communicate telepathically and manifest one's needs, are the natural abilities that mankind possessed eons ago, only this time, these faculties are all the more evolved in importance now mankind has experienced existence without them. How much easier life would have been during these past many centuries had humanity retained these faculties!

That is a lesson learned. It is as if our souls had been blindfolded and bound to walk without eyes. We had to rely on reason and the rational mind, on science and technology, to see through the haze of existence. So the "blind", the Fifth Root-Race, must lead those with vision into revolutionary modes of New Golden Age education.

Pre-knowledge in the New Race

Another aspect of learning will involve the understanding and dissemination of pre-knowledge embedded in the souls of Sixth Root-Race incarnations. Sixth Root-Race children have been streaming into incarnation since the mid-1940's with the greatest numbers arriving from the 1960s onward. By the time the transitional society comes into action, Sixth Root-Race incarnations will range in age from the sixties down. Some of those born from 1970 onward bear knowledge in their souls that will be pertinent to the building of the transitional society.

Throughout their lives in the pre-2012 era they have felt "different" and detached from society because there was something buried deep inside that could not be expressed. Adepts using proper meditative techniques or key sounds will trigger their souls to release this knowledge, and the individual will find a store of knowledge that was always intuitively there. Some of this knowledge involves technologies from higher evolutions, which will help Spiritual Regions adapt more quickly to their situations.

The Spiritual Hierarchy planned this "triggered" pre-knowledge as a way to create order out of chaos, especially when other priorities of rebuilding would take precedence over the educational function of society.

4. Marriage and Balancing Masculine and Feminine Energies

One of the main tasks of the transitional society will be to balance the masculine and feminine energies. This balance comes as a result of Soul Liberation, for within the soul these energies are perfectly balanced. So the masculine-feminine balance must be achieved individually, and this balance will naturally carry over into group activity. *The balance has little to do with gender: it is a matter of soul manifestation.* To "genderize" the current inflow of feminine energies is to fall into the same trap that the dominant masculine energies of our times have fallen into.

As masculine and feminine energies come into equilibrium, marriage as conceived in our present civilisation will eventually fade out. This trend already started a few decades ago. Instead of a physical man and woman in marriage representing the balance between the male and female energies, the male-female balance will occur within each individual as the true nature of the soul manifests through either the male or female body vehicles. This rebalancing is already happening in a large sector of the spiritual community. In the transitional society, pairing or grouping of individuals will manifest according to the Law of Attraction, one balanced soul with another or several balanced souls together.

However, certain responsibilities need to be defined for couples who bear children. Here is an opportunity for the transitional society to define both parental and societal responsibilities because of the obvious need for a renewal of the race with incoming souls. The decision to bear children, in other words, may be subject to broader decisions outside the narrow limits of the family nucleus. The family nucleus of this era will not carry over into the New Golden Age but will give way to a more extended group family, perhaps like the experiments of the kibbutz communities and the flower children in the 1960's but in a more organized and less chaotic manner.

5. Spiritual Life and Religion

The Spiritual Regions will be freed from most of the astral *maya* that created separate warring religions on earth. These religions, along with the unaffiliated, will come to the realization that at the origin of all their beliefs is the Ageless Wisdom. Their esoteric branches, i.e. Sufis, Vajrayana, Gnostics, etc. have already come to this conclusion.

Those arriving in the Spiritual Regions will readily embrace cosmic laws and let go former religious beliefs in favour of the more ecumenical teachings of the Ageless Wisdom. This may be one of the most difficult transitions that church-affiliated members in the Spiritual Regions will make. In short, there will be no denominational religion in the Spiritual Regions because spirituality will be interwoven into society's very fabric.

For quite some time, an etheric committee of the Spiritual Hierarchy has been working to meld all the teachings of these early religions into a one world spiritual teaching. The committee members, former church officials, all came to the realization upon their deaths, that what they had been preaching on the earth plane was not quite right, and in the spirit of righting these teachings in conformity to cosmic laws and principles elicited in the Ageless Wisdom, they formed this working committee. Their labour of love will serve as preparation for the coming world teacher.

Life Motivations

Life in the Spiritual Regions will be motivated by a deeper desire to serve. Living for the acquisition of material goods, power, or pleasures will no longer satisfy survivors. Something higher must motivate them. There will be no shopping centres, no endless streams of electronic entertainment, no more wars for money and power and no more industries to titillate the senses. Life will be fairly basic and mankind will appreciate once again the small things in life. The bloom of the rosebud, the rising and setting of the sun, nature's way of communicating with mankind, will once again stimulate a co-partnership between mankind and its host, the earth.

The desire for more knowledge within a framework of cosmic law will again resound in our souls—the I AM within. Knowledge that awakens latent knowledge—discovery-- is very much part of Soul Liberation and should drive the individual to search and search for more. All will have access to this bountiful knowledge and to the wisdom of any teacher

they wish. An individual need only ask and have a deep desire to know, and the right teacher and circumstances will present themselves, either physically or etherically. The pure and simple desire to know, the discovery, and then the satisfaction of understanding will lead to the manifestation of knowledge in life. Spiritual progression and evolution will again become the main
vectors of life.

Epilogue
Soul Liberation

We have focussed on the lightbearers in this book primarily because they represent the most important yet weakest link in the overall pralaya strategy of the Spiritual Hierarchy. Their healing role in the economic and political crisis upon us, their humanitarian actions during the Great Floods of the lowland and coastal areas, and their leadership in laying building blocks for a Golden Age will be essential to the survival of our present civilisation.

Many lightbearers have already completed the retrieval of their initiation levels and are well on the road to preparing themselves for the challenging tasks ahead. However, the majority of the lightbearers languish in indecision borne of selfishness and fear.

Prior to this incarnation, we eagerly volunteered for this incarnation, because we saw the glorious Plan for this era and its ultimate goal of Soul Liberation. Our souls saw something so marvellous that we interrupted our personal spiritual quest on the Path in order to come back and help humanity in its time of greatest need. We all saw that life in the Spiritual Regions would finally enable the soul to express itself through an ever finer physical personality without the fetters of the economic, financial and banking, political and social systems and boundaries. We could see together how a reconstructed civilisation would spread throughout the world on an entirely different footing, and the chance to rebuild civilisation on firmer spiritual foundations was so compelling that we seized the opportunity to come back because otherwise there would be no hope left for the human race we loved so much.

We also saw that the key restraint that has so blocked humanity's evolution was going to be eliminated once and for all. "What an opportunity to set things right again!" we declared. The pralaya would take place and down would come all shackles the Dark Forces had built around humanity. We saw the inevitable crumbling of their systems as earth washed out the old, in preparation for the new cycle, and this gave us even more hope to set the course of humanity's evolution on the right footing.

We now have an idea what to expect. The times ahead will not be easy and only a stalwart commitment to your soul purpose and mission will get you through the turmoil and chaos of the pralaya. Then will follow the rigors of working with the Spiritual Hierarchy, for there is no compromise on the quality it seeks from lightbearers. Their goal is that mankind can finally release the soul's potential through the material form in order to demonstrate what marvels it can create, individually and collectively, on earth. This is the essence of Soul Liberation.

If you still share this overall vision of the world, a New Golden Age of liberated souls, then you have but to commit to the Divine Plan that will make it happen. This is still a matter of choice.

TIMETABLE OF EVENTS

2005 –2012

- Severe worldwide economic and financial crisis
- Armageddon/filtering process continues at heightened vibrations: general insanity
- World economy hits bottom and stays there. All conventional efforts to revive it fail
- World War III starts to keep people working
- Water related catastrophes: tsunamis, hurricanes, rise in sea level, floods of lowland and coastal areas due to meltdown of icecaps at the poles and the permafrost areas of the world
- Spiritual Regions on higher ground begin to develop: initial preparations

2013–2020

- Water-related catastrophes multiply making more and more of the low-lying areas uninhabitable
- Massive population displacements to higher ground
- Spiritual Regions take hold as lightbearers find their way there
- Period of Reconstruction: Transitional societies begin to consolidate in the Spiritual Regions

2021-2080

- Transitional Societies continue to consolidate in each Spiritual Region experimenting with various modes of organisation, the cosmic laws

- World Teacher's principles pour down on the Spiritual Regions and become common bond among them
- Indications of major continental shifts, rifts, and movements begin to perturb the earth's surface
- Spiritual Regions become more physically isolated from each other due to the earth changes, although they remain linked etherically

Bibliography

Bailey, Alice A. *A Treatise on White Magic or the Way of the Disciple*, New York: Lucis Publishing Company, 1934.

_____*Initiation Human and Solar*, New York: Lucis Publishing Company, 1922.

_____*Telepathy and the Etheric Vehicle*, New York: Lucis Publishing Company, 1950.

_____*The Externalisation of the Hierarchy*, New York: Lucis Publishing Company, 1957.

_____*A Treatise on Cosmic Fire*, New York: Lucis Publishing Company, 1925.

Clow, Barbara Hand, *The Pleiadian Agenda*, Santa Fe, New Mexico: Bear and Co. Publishing, 1995

Cranston, Sylvia, *Helena Blavatsky—Founder of the Modern Theosophical Movement,* Santa Barbara: Path Publishing House, 1993

Innocenti, Geraldine, *Bridge to Freedom Collection of Channelings*, 1953

King, Godfre Ray (G. Ballard), *The Magic Presence*, Schaumburg, Illinois: Saint Germain Press, Inc., 1935

_____, *The Unveiled Mysteries*, Schaumburg, Illinois: Saint Germain Press, Inc., 1982

Leadbeater, C.W. *The Inner Life, vol. 1*, Adyar, India: The Theosophical Publishing House, 1910.

Olcott, Henry Steele, *Old Diary Leaves Vol. 1*, Adyar, India: The Theosophical Publishing House, 1900

Powell, A.E., *The Astral Body and Other Astral Phenomena*, Adyar (Chennai) India: The Theosophical Publishing House, 1927

_____, *The Mental Body*, Adyar (Chennai) India: The Theosophical Publishing House, 2000

_____, *The Etheric Double*, Adyar (Chennai) India: The Theosophical Publishing House, 1925

Printz, Thomas, *The First Ray*, Bridge to Freedom, Mt. Shasta: Ascended Master Teaching Foundation, 1953.

Sinnett, A.P, *The Mahatma Letters to A.P. Sinnett*, Adyar, India: Theosophical Publishing House

_____*Esoteric Budhism (sic)*, Reprinted by San Diego: Wizard Bookshelf, 1994

"The Heat is On," Special in the *Economist,* vol.380, no. 8494. 9-15 September, 2006

"It Rained in Antarctica this Winter," *La Presse de Montreal*, April, 2006

Breinigsville, PA USA
17 January 2011
253480BV00003B/55/P

Breinigsville, PA USA
17 January 2011
253480BV00003B/55/P